STILL TOO SEXY

SURVIVING RIGHT SAID FRED

RICHARD AND FRED FAIRBRASS WITH JOEL MCIVER

OMNIBUS PRESS

Copyright © 2022 Omnibus Press
(A division of the Wise Music Group
14–15 Berners Street, London, W1T 3LJ)

Cover design by Paul Tippett.

Picture research by Fred and Richard Fairbrass.

ISBN 978-1-9131-7250-3
Signed edition ISBN 978-1-9131-7292-3

Every effort has been made to trace the copyright holders of
the photographs in this book but one or two were unreachable.
We would be grateful if the photographers concerned would
contact us.

A catalogue record for this book is available from the British Library.

Typeset by Evolution Design & Digital Ltd (Kent)
Printed in Malta.
www.omnibuspress.com

Contents

Foreword

I first met Fred and Richard of Right Said Fred back in the early nineties, in a famous nightclub, Browns, in London. I remember it being not long after 'I'm Too Sexy' was released around 1991, and I wanted to congratulate them on their successful release.

We started chatting about our very different careers: there was a mutual respect for our journeys and achievements. After that we saw each other over the years on the circuit and at different events, and became friends despite the busy schedules we all had. I love straight talkers, I love honest and raw people: I saw this in both of them – and I still have a real love for 'I'm Too Sexy'. It's such a classic.

We didn't see each other for some time until last year, when we were all involved in a mental health event for Gibraltar: we're advocates in this particular area. It was like old times all over again, apart from 'We haven't aged'... We stayed in touch and picked up our friendship where we left off.

I wish them every success in all their forthcoming adventures. I look forward to sharing it with them, and I can't wait to read their autobiography and go to the pub for a pint.

Right Said Fred will always be iconic.

Eddie Kidd OBE
2022

Introduction

Welcome to our book, and thank you for buying it, borrowing it or stealing it. However you acquired it, you're reading it – and we appreciate that.

We wrote this book in 2021 and '22, partly because the pandemic forced us to down tools and we couldn't go on tour. The upside of that situation, even though it's been miserable for everyone, is that it's allowed us to reflect on where we've been, where we are and where we're going.

As you'll see, our story has been chaotic, with a lot of mental damage inflicted and shady business dealings executed along the way – but we've made a great deal of music that a lot of people like, which was all we ever wanted. We've included the lyrics of nine songs that mean something to us, to allow you a look inside our creative process, but we haven't overthought it: it's only pop'n'roll, after all.

This book is a conversation between the two of us, recorded over a period of about a week in the summer of 2021. It is therefore not in strict chronological order. Additions have been made along the way, and you'll also see that certain key moments have been indicated with the words 'Survival Tip'. After all, this book is about survival.

God knows how we made it out alive, but somehow we did. Let's hope for better times ahead.

With love...

Richard Fairbrass
Fred Fairbrass
Windsor, England
2022

Chapter 1

Early Doors

We were young. We were frustrated.
We were looking for more.

RICH: This is the childhood chapter, I suppose. How the fuck are we supposed to remember that far back?

FRED: Just give it a go. What's your earliest memory?

RICH: My earliest memory has probably had repercussions throughout my life. I remember sitting in a chair in our Aunt Lucy's house. She had a beautiful house down on the south coast. I had no clothes on because I'd just had a bath, so I was just sitting there, and Lucy came in and said, 'Close your legs. Don't sit like that.' That's a strange thing to say to a three-year-old, isn't it? What about you?

FRED: My earliest memory is being knocked off my potty by our dog, Chloe. I remember that quite clearly. And the other thing I remember quite well is my pusher. For anyone who doesn't know what that is, instead of a knife and fork, you had a knife and pusher, which looked like the front of a bulldozer. I also remember Mum having me on reins as well, when I was two or three years old.

RICH: I think you should still be on reins. For the record, our mum was called Betty Fairbrass and our dad was Peter Abbott Fairbrass.

FRED: They were good parents.

RICH: Yes, I think we had a pretty great upbringing. We grew up in the countryside, and we had a healthy diet, didn't we? There was no microwave cooking or anything, because Mum cooked everything fresh and Dad grew a lot of his own vegetables. We cycled to school. We were very clean-living.

FRED: The other thing I remember is that, because Dad was a print salesman, in the early days he used to come home with lots of bound books. All the pages were blank, because they were test runs or something, and he would bring them home and I would use them as sketchbooks. I remember drawing trains and submarines and things. I was probably about four.

RICH: We should probably tell the readers when and where we were born.

FRED: Go on then.

RICH: I was born on 22 September 1953, in hospital at Kingston-upon-Thames, but I don't remember where we lived at the time.

FRED: I was born on 2 November 1956, in Penge, in the same hospital that Mick Jagger was born in. My name is actually Christopher Fairbrass, but everybody calls me Fred because when I was at primary school, one of the kids called himself 'Captain Brobat Fantastic' for reasons I've long forgotten. I got called 'Freddie Fabulous', and the Fred stuck.

RICH: I've never called you Chris, although Mum sometimes did. We just got used to calling you Fred. Anyway, I think Fred suits you better than Chris.

FRED: I think so too. By the way, my birth certificate says that I was born in Dartford. I don't know why that is. Do you?

RICH: I don't know either, and unfortunately there's no one left to ask. I do know that, way back, we lived in a very small, terraced house which was out towards Surbiton in south-west London.

Then we moved to East Grinstead in Sussex in the very late fifties. The house was brand new, and we grew up there. It was a three-bedroom house with an acre of ground, and it cost £3,000. I couldn't have been more than about five or six when we moved to East Grinstead, because I went straight to the primary school. You would have been three or four, something like that.

FRED: Why did we move to East Grinstead?

RICH: I think Mum and Dad just wanted to upgrade, you know. That house was named Abbottswood after Dad's middle name Abbott, and it was where we lived until we moved to London in 1981.

FRED: During a fight with you I cut my head on a door handle, so I was rushed off to hospital, and on the way back a neighbour flagged us down to tell us that John F. Kennedy had been assassinated. That means it was 22 November 1963, and I'd just turned seven. I remember the TV was rubbish that night: it was all very depressing.

RICH: We were middle-middle class.

FRED: Definitely not upper-middle class, though.

RICH: No, although at the time I think I wished we were. I remember once we went on a camping holiday, and Dad put all these collapsible chairs on the roof of the car. I remember thinking, 'This is fucking embarrassing. Everybody knows we can't afford a fucking hotel.'

FRED: Did we enjoy camping? I can't remember.

RICH: I absolutely hated camping. Those holidays didn't give Mum enough of a break, because she was still having to cook for us all. I thought we might as well stay at home.

FRED: I think I enjoyed camping. I suppose I was a bit younger than you and didn't think about things as much.

RICH: Well, it got a bit stressful sometimes. We went camping on one occasion, and the groundsheet in the tent was rucked up. Mum was carrying a colander of hot spaghetti and tripped over

3

the groundsheet, so some of the spaghetti went on the floor. Dad was sitting in a chair and didn't get up to help – perhaps he didn't think it was his place to do so. Mum was furious, and she tipped the remainder of the spaghetti in the colander over his head! From that moment on, Dad got the message.

FRED: We used to go on foreign holidays as well, though. We went to Sardinia and Ibiza.

RICH: The only reason we could do that was because the company Dad worked for printed travel brochures, so we got a really good deal on the holidays. If it wasn't for that, we couldn't have afforded it.

FRED: You and I were quite different kids, I think.

RICH: Probably because the three years between us meant a lot when we were little, so we weren't close straight away. I was more bookish, and you were more into going out and being a bit of a lad. I remember once you came in and said, 'I've got this great money-making scheme – it's brilliant.' So I said, 'What is it?' and you said, 'There's a telephone box at the top of our street – let's just take all the money from that!'

FRED: I thought, 'There's a box full of money here. Why don't we just rip it apart?'

RICH: That was a shit idea. It was music that really brought us together. That happened when we were in our early to mid-teens, I guess.

FRED: We had very different sets of friends before that.

RICH: I didn't have many friends! I was more interested in assembling Airfix models. Being a lead singer was never what I planned.

FRED: We both failed the 11-plus exam. I still don't know why, because we were reasonably clever.

RICH: I remember I couldn't bring myself to tell Dad that I'd failed, so I went and told him, 'I passed, but there are no spaces at the grammar school.' But he said, 'If you've passed, you deserve to go to grammar school. I'm going to have a word with them.' So now I'm thinking, 'Oh fuck! Now I'm in the shit,' and of course, he ultimately found out.

FRED: Did you get into trouble?

RICH: No, he didn't care. I should have told him the truth straight away.

FRED: So why didn't you?

RICH: I sensed that he was very old-fashioned, I guess. He'd had a miserable time in private school when he was younger, so I think he had quite high ambitions for me, academically.

FRED: Dad never even asked me about the 11-plus result. He assumed I'd failed, because I was a bit troublesome, and I was much more into sports than studying. Football was my passion.

RICH: I remember you being really good at it.

FRED: I suppose I was, because I was scouted by Chelsea and Fulham. I wasn't quite good enough for them, but I did play at county level. When I was 13, I was playing with the over-15s as a striker. I was on the left wing because I was good with both feet. I'm a little bit ambidextrous, so I could cross with my left foot, and then go inside and shoot with my right.

RICH: You wanted to play football as a career, didn't you?

FRED: I was hoping to, although I don't think I could have done it because I wasn't good enough, but I trained all the time and I played matches every Saturday. I had a football goal in the garden where I would train by myself. I took it all quite seriously.

RICH: Dad loved football too.

FRED: Yes, it became a bond between us. Dad would come and see me play a lot. I won medals, and I was the team's top scorer for a couple of seasons running, and I was even written about a little bit in the local press. Mind you, as soon as I started learning the guitar, football took a back seat. I suddenly thought, 'This is what I want to do with my life.'

It was a lot to do with people's personalities. I liked the musicians that I met, and I didn't gel as well with the blokes I was playing football with. The other reason I gave up football was that I was ill for a year between 13 and 14 with glandular fever.

RICH: Oh, I remember that. You were really ill.

FRED: I was. I was completely isolated – it was like being in lockdown. The school sent somebody to our house to make sure that our parents weren't just letting me play truant. My mum said, 'You can't come in. He's got glandular fever,' so I spoke to the guy through the window. Anyway, I missed almost a whole year of secondary school, which was Imberhorne School in East Grinstead, and that changed my mindset somehow. After that I became quite troubled. I got into a lot of disagreements, mostly with teachers.

RICH: Why do you think that was?

FRED: I think I came out of the illness feeling angry, because I was behind a year, I couldn't catch up and I felt really isolated. So I started to play up, and I got into trouble at school. I remember I was in an English Constitution exam, and a sports teacher came in and said, 'You're wasting your time in here, Fairbrass. We need you to play football for the school.' I was expelled when I was 15.

RICH: Remind me what for?

FRED: I had an argument with a teacher, so I went and got a football and kicked it through the window of his office. He was covered in glass, and I was then expelled. I can't say I blame him.

RICH: Yes, that would do it. He was a bit strange, wasn't he? Didn't they find him dancing nearly naked at the lunchtime disco? I think he was subsequently suspended.

FRED: A lot of them were a bit weird, and they weren't exactly encouraging either.

RICH: Secondary schools deliberately inculcated a sense of failure back then.

FRED: I was practising my guitar in break once, and a teacher told me, 'You can't make a living doing that.' I replied, 'Paul McCartney does,' and he hit me round the head. I just thought, 'Well, if you think I can't make it, I bet I can.'

RICH: It was a rough kind of school, Imberhorne. It was a secondary school, so it was before the comprehensive schools policy came in. You could cheat the system quite easily if you knew how. I won an art competition by tracing a Salvador Dali picture. I remember thinking, 'Okay, there's a way to do this.' I couldn't believe they didn't spot it. It says a lot about them.

FRED: Your art teacher couldn't have been that bright. Some of the boys at Imberhorne had been sent down to our school from Borstal in Sunderland and Newcastle. Our school was used as their gateway back into society. They could be terrifying. I remember one of them stabbed a kid through the foot with a javelin.

RICH: The teacher came in holding a white plimsoll, which was red with blood, and held it under our noses as a lesson to be careful with javelins.

FRED: I was a bit of a handful myself. I stabbed a kid in the hand with a pen once, although that sounds worse than it was. We were just playing around. Mum and Dad seemed to accept that maybe I was just different to you. I wasn't a bad pupil, really: I was quite good at English language and literature.

RICH: You tried out a couple of schools before Imberhorne, if I remember correctly.

FRED: I did, yeah. Around the age of 10 or 11, I was sent to Whitfield, a private school, to do the entrance exam, but when I

7

found out that they played rugby and not football, I sat there and refused to do it. They told Dad, 'Your son hasn't got in.' There was another school I tried out for as well, at Hurstpierpoint in Sussex. It was the same thing – they only played rugby – so I just sat in the classroom and doodled on the entrance exam. And that was it.

RICH: Shocker! I was really fed up after the 11-plus exam, because our group of friends from primary school had all split up. Some of our friends went to grammar school, and some didn't. I quite fancied one of the guys who went to secondary school with me, but it wasn't reciprocated.

FRED: You dirty Bertie.

RICH: I remember being shocked that we didn't have separate cubicles in the shower. I remember thinking, 'This won't do at all.'

FRED: You were a little bit of a snob, weren't you?

RICH: I was, I suppose. Talking of the showers, one guy always used to get a huge hard-on in the shower. He was about the same age as the rest of us, around 12 or 13, but even at that age, he had a penis the size of my leg. I shall never forget it.

FRED: Life isn't fair.

RICH: I remember thinking that the idea that God makes us all equal is an absolute bloody joke.

FRED: On the subject of God, we were very sceptical about religion.

RICH: Yeah, as was Dad. I sometimes think that he might have been abused in school, not physically but emotionally.

FRED: We think Mum was of Jewish extraction, but religion never played a major role in our family. I think that our kind of non-religious family might have been a bit strange in East Grinstead at the time.

RICH: Yes, it was a really strong Conservative area. The local Conservatives paid for a day at the Royal Tournament for all the kids of Tory voters, which was their way of staying in their good books. I went on a couple of trips courtesy of the local Tory party.

FRED: Did we have any dealings at all with the church?

RICH: No, and to give you an idea of what the Church of England was like back then, when we first moved into the area, the local vicar knocked on our door and asked why we weren't going to service. That would never happen nowadays.

FRED: Mind you, East Grinstead does have its share of unorthodox religions. The British Church of Scientology has its HQ there.

RICH: The Mormon Temple is in East Grinstead too. I remember once we jumped over the fence and went into the grounds, because we wanted to find a place to snog our girlfriends. It was pitch-black, and I thought I was fondling this girl's boob, but it was her fucking elbow. I swear that's a true story. The groundsman came out and chased us away.

FRED: Should we talk about Mum and Dad a bit?

RICH: Yes, I think we should.

FRED: Mum told us she wanted to be a singer and dancer when she was young. She was raised by a single mother without a pot to piss in.

RICH: After the war, she got married to Dad and became a housewife, but she would have loved to be a singer and dancer. She took singing lessons when she was a kid. As it did for a lot of people back then, the war just took away any dreams that she had. I think the reason that people are so relaxed now about the rights they have is because they've never had to fight for them.

FRED: There was a military barracks called Hobbs Barracks near East Grinstead, and a film company hired the place to make a film about concentration camps in the Second World

9

War. Mum got a job there as a secretary. That gave her a little taste of the thing that she always wanted – a bit of showbiz. Dad didn't like it, because he was from a generation that felt that the husband was the breadwinner. If his wife was going out to make money, what that implied was that he wasn't making enough money. But Mum was absolutely determined. She needed people, and she liked company. She didn't want to be stuck in the house all the time.

RICH: During the Second World War, Dad had been in the Merchant Navy. He was on a minesweeper in the Atlantic, and later transferred to the west coast of Italy for Combined Operations. I think that made him quite tightly wound. There's an amazing story, actually. His brother Jack was also in the war, and his ship went down. As far as Dad was concerned, Jack was dead, but some months later he was in a bar in Canada. He heard this whistle, which he immediately recognised, and it belonged to Jack. Dad didn't know that he'd been transferred just before the sinking.

FRED: I love that story. Jack was a nice guy.

RICH: He was a great tennis player too. Do you remember, when you and I were in our teens, we both played a bit of tennis, and he said, 'Oh, I'll give you a game.' We both thought, 'This is silly – we'll slaughter him.' He said, 'You two both go on that side, and I'll play you from this side.' He then absolutely hammered us. That was a reminder that youth isn't everything.

FRED: Jack and Dad would have made a fortune if they'd worked together in printing, but they didn't get on, in business at least. They just didn't see eye to eye, although personally they got on fine.

RICH: Dad came from a wealthy family, although the money had all gone by the time we came along. I think it made him very ambitious, but also the thing that curbed his ambition financially was his love of family. He was offered a job in America in the mid- to late sixties, and it was a really well-paid job, a big promotion for him. I remember thinking, 'This is going to be great!' but he turned it down, because his family was in the UK. I thought, 'What the hell? You silly sod,' but again, now I get it.

FRED: That would have been a bit of a different environment to East Grinstead.

RICH: Just a bit. Do you remember, there was a kid who came to live with us at our house because his parents were divorcing? He and I started messing around, like you do at 14. That went on, on and off, for several years.

FRED: Did our parents know about it? I assume they didn't.

RICH: I don't know. When you're a kid, you tend to think your mum and dad are really stupid, and you hide the truth and you think you're brilliant, but truthfully, they know what's going on.

FRED: True. Was it tough to be a gay teenager back then?

RICH: Well, back then you had clusters of intolerance. It's a whole lot better now, but certainly back in the mid-seventies through to the early nineties, it was really rough, not that I really thought about it much when I was 14. When did we get the music bug?

FRED: Our first exposure to that came from the Dean Martin and Trini Lopez records that our parents had. Later, a couple that our parents knew went abroad and left their entire record collection for Mum and Dad to look after, so we listened to Motown, The Rolling Stones, the Yardbirds and a whole lot more. We got into singer-songwriters when we went on holiday to Italy in 1970, when I was 14 and you were 17. We stayed at a villa that was owned by a friend of Dad's, on the edge of Lake Bracciano. The weather was pretty bad, but fortunately they had two records in the house, which were Simon & Garfunkel's

Bridge Over Troubled Water and *Nashville Skyline* by Bob Dylan. I played them back to back, endlessly. I thought Dylan was a fucking master. I just loved his lyrics.

RICH: We'd listened to the Stones and The Beatles way before that, of course. Do you remember that time we saw Paul McCartney? When we were kids, we had an old Humber Sceptre, and we had a guitar cabinet in the boot. The boot lid wouldn't come down properly, so we had it tied down. This Rolls-Royce came flying past us down a country lane, and it was Paul and Linda McCartney, hooting and waving at us.

FRED: Years later, we were in Nomis Studios at Olympia in London, and Paul and Linda were there. We started talking, and I was eating a chicken sandwich. He said, 'I need to talk to you about that,' so I flexed my bicep and said, 'Look at me, and look at you.' We had a laugh about that. He had his violin bass, and we were chatting about that while Linda helped to make the tea. They were very nice people. I can see why he fell for her, because she was very easy to chat to. I was struck by how nice she was.

RICH: I was out at lunch and fucking missed them.

FRED: One of the first LPs I bought was *Disraeli Gears* by Cream. I think it's one of my favourite guitar performances.

RICH: We liked Elvis Presley too. The thing that struck me about Elvis was that he was really sexual. Even if he hadn't been a great singer, you'd hire him as a model. The reality is that some guys are really beautiful. Deal with it.

FRED: I remember we played *Deep Purple In Rock* again and again, and we were really into glam too – T. Rex, early David Bowie, Sweet and the rest of them. Elvis was a game-changer for me too, but you were always more into Frank Sinatra.

RICH: The first time I really got into a vocal performance was Frank Sinatra's 'New York, New York'. The way he growls into the key change at the end really stuck with me.

FRED: I was a massive fan of Fleetwood Mac as a kid, particularly the Peter Green stuff. I loved the album *The Pious Bird of Good Omen*. In fact, I was so obsessed with them that I got on the phone to their record company.

RICH: Why?

FRED: Fuck knows. I think I wanted to ask them when they were touring or something. I ended up speaking to some people at a recording studio after the record company gave me the number. They must have found it amusing. I remember them laughing because they had some young kid on the phone.

RICH: Around this time we listened to all sorts of music. Dean Martin, Frank Sinatra, the Stones, The Beatles, Cream and Creedence Clearwater Revival. Then, as we got into the early seventies, we moved on to Deep Purple, Led Zeppelin, David Bowie, T. Rex, Sweet, Roxy Music, Lou Reed and others.

FRED: We started going to gigs in the late sixties, or maybe the very early seventies. We saw Stray, Arthur Brown, Wings, T. Rex, Roxy Music, Flash, Brinsley Schwarz, Alice Cooper, Pink Floyd, Joe Cocker, David Bowie and Barclay James Harvest. Not a bad list, is it?

RICH: That's a great list of bands, but actually I was more interested in acting than music at this point. It was what I wanted to do when I was a kid, so I did school productions and stuff. I remember I had to learn something from *The Wind in the Willows*. It was a really long monologue, and I remember thinking, 'There's no way I'm ever going to remember this. I'm never going to be an actor.'

FRED: It wasn't long before I decided to pick up the guitar, and pretty soon I became obsessed with it. I played it so often that I even stopped seeing my mates. Standing around in a pub, drinking beer, trying to chat up some local girls wasn't my thing.

RICH: Did you think of music as a possible career?

FRED: I did, although I had no idea how you actually went about making that a reality. I took guitar lessons, and in the first lesson the teacher, Mr Prentice, said, 'I'm guessing classical guitar isn't going to be your area,' and showed me some Big Bill Broonzy blues licks.

RICH: Good advice.

FRED: I got a bunch of Beatles and Motown books, and played a bit of Bob Dylan and whatever, and started to make some progress. I don't think our parents really understood what I was doing or why I was doing it, though.

RICH: Dad didn't think that music was a way to make a living, and that it wasn't to be taken too seriously, but he was very libertarian, I guess – do what you want to do.

FRED: He thought that we would give up music and settle down and go to farming college or something. I suppose, if the band hadn't worked out, we would have ended up running a gym. At the same time, though, Dad didn't like authority, and we're both like him in that sense. Although he was very conservative, he had an underlying mistrust of the church, politicians and the police. He didn't hate them, and he didn't think they were all bad, but he kept his distance from them, and I think we inherited that. The reason why I'm saying this is because that sense of rebellion stayed with us when we became successful independent musicians.

RICH: After you got into guitar, I wanted to get into playing music too, so I bought a bass.

FRED: Well, it is the easy option.

RICH: I had no ambition to be in music, but when you started on guitar, you would play me bits and pieces of what you were doing. It was slightly Machiavellian of me, I suppose, because I remember thinking, 'I might want to hitch my flag to his music, because it's not bad.'

FRED: 'Not bad'? What a huge compliment.

RICH: I don't really know why I chose bass, specifically. You know how some people buy wine just because they like the label? I only bought the bass because I liked the look of it. I also thought, 'It's only got four strings – it's got to be easier than guitar.'

FRED: Neither of us knew what the hell we were doing, really. Some people still think we don't.

RICH: I didn't even have a bass amp, because I didn't think you needed one. I played everything on the D and G strings above the tenth fret, because you can't hear anything below that.

FRED: Eventually we bought an amp head for the bass, but it still didn't make any noise. We went back and complained, and the guy explained that we needed a cabinet too. We were so naive.

RICH: I really tried to listen to the bass parts in the songs I loved, in order to get better at it. When it comes to bassists that I admire, I loved Andy Fraser of Free, and Paul McCartney's bass part on 'Come Together' always stayed with me. Ronnie Lane's playing on the Faces' 'Stay With Me' was an object lesson too. The bass is mixed high in that track, because the band obviously knew that it was a major part of the appeal of that particular song. His part is really, really melodic.

FRED: True, that.

RICH: Because we had no money for amps, we wrote a letter to a guy at the top of our road called Fred Kobler. He was the local millionaire and lived in a great big house called Baldwyns. I think he made his money from hotels, and I think he was on the board of Watney's, the brewing company.

FRED: I remember that. We wrote him a letter saying, 'Can you please lend us £200 so we can buy some amps?' He wrote back and said, 'I'm a Czech refugee. I arrived in the UK with nothing. I've earned every penny that I have, but I'm looking for two gardeners, so why don't you come up here and earn some money?' So we went up there and worked for him as leaf sweepers for a year or two.

RICH: His gardens were done out in a kind of Japanese style, weren't they? Beautifully kept.

FRED: I think he paid us 30p an hour.

RICH: While we were working there, we saw this very pretty guy walking around, wearing jodhpurs and with rouge on his cheeks. The way he moved was very fluid and graceful. We thought that he might be Fred Kobler's boyfriend.

FRED: Fred was a nice bloke, wasn't he?

RICH: He was. Many years after that, when I was with my partner Stuart and he had become HIV positive, we went to the Chelsea and Westminster Hospital, and the HIV centre there is called the Kobler Outpatient Clinic. When Fred Kobler died, he left money to this clinic. I went in there when Stuart was having a blood test, and there was this picture of Fred Kobler on the wall. I remember looking at the picture and thinking, 'I know that face.' That wheel came full circle.

Survival Tip No. 1: Know the Value of Money

RICH: He lent us money to buy some wellington boots for the garden work, and when we stopped working for him, we just left them in our garage because we didn't think he would want them back. Anyway, he eventually knocked on our door and said, 'Can I have my boots back?' And I remember thinking, 'You silly old sod. What do you want these old boots for?' But now, of course, I get it. They weren't ours. He was quite right.

FRED: We learned a lot from him, specifically about the value of money. We didn't make enough money to buy the amps, though. I think Dad got those for us, didn't he?

RICH: Yes. The company he worked for started printing brochures for Marshall Amplification, so we got two 100-watt stacks – not given to us for free, but very cheap. Just a tad loud for a bedroom. I wish I'd kept them, because they'd be worth a fortune now.

FRED: Many thousands, probably. That was good of Dad to do that.

RICH: We were lucky; he was really supportive. I remember he once carted a bloody huge Takamine acoustic guitar on the train all the way back from London for you.

FRED: I still have that guitar. So we now had amps, a guitar and a bass, and we could really work on our playing. I think we made pretty fast progress, now I come to think of it.

RICH: We both became reasonably decent musicians before long. I dug deep into bass. I remember that I discovered a track on the first Paul McCartney album called 'Momma Miss America'. He plays an octave line on that song, and that was a real awakening for me as to how the bass can colour a track if you want it to. You can either sit in the back and play the groove, or you can change the nature of where the emphasis is. The other important thing is that I'm left-handed, but I play right-handed, which means that my fretting hand is strong, but my picking hand is not very effective. It's partly because I don't have a very strong picking hand that I play melodically.

FRED: Around 1970, when I was in my early teens and you were leaving school, it was starting to become obvious that neither of us really fitted in in East Grinstead. The music we listened to wasn't what everyone else was listening to, and also you were half a poof.

RICH: At that time and place, people were looking to get jobs in local firms or to teach locally, all that sort of stuff. I think because we were quite insistent about playing music, we stopped fitting in.

FRED: Did you leave home for a while?

RICH: I didn't actually leave home, but I slept in a car park on and off for a few months. I don't really know why, but I know I was really unhappy at home for some reason. Obviously, I wanted something different from life, but I didn't know what it was. I remember sleeping up against the wheel of a car, and the only thing that woke me up was when the guy got in the car and drove off.

FRED: Yes, I remember that.

RICH: I can't remember how many times I did it, but I know it was more than once.

FRED: Did Mum and Dad say anything about it?

RICH: No. I think they were probably pretty worried, but they didn't let on. They may have discussed it between themselves.

FRED: Well, it was a strange time. School was crap, and when we left, the jobs we did were pretty terrible too.

RICH: I think the whole sleeping-outside thing was to do with not knowing how to change that – like, 'How the fuck do I get out of this?'

FRED: Did you feel happier after you left Imberhorne?

RICH: To an extent. I then worked in a company called Hellerman Deutsch, as an accountant's clerk. The only thing I remember about that place was a Welsh girl called Moira, who I had a sort of romance with, sitting on the photocopier and photocopying her arse. I liked her because she did that kind of thing. After that I went to Crawley Technical College to do A-Levels, but got poor grades, so I went to night school to repeat one of them. Sometime later, I started a degree course in humanities at East London Polytechnic, but dropped out to focus on music.

FRED: I worked in a timber yard, and I really hated it. I had to lift the sides of sheds into a warehouse. I didn't last long there because I got sick to death of the splinters in my head. Another time, I had a job cleaning out a warehouse which was full of rotten watermelons. When I went in there, all I could see were wasps. You literally could not see anything because of the wasps in the air, and when you picked up a watermelon they instantly burst. It was fucking disgusting. Mind you, I always got a seat on the underground going home because I stank of rotten fruit. Fortunately I got a job at Gray's Record Shop in East Grinstead, which I loved. It introduced me to shitloads of new music.

RICH: That was a great job for you. We also started working in London around this time.

FRED: We did. I got a job at a shop called Moonshine in Hampstead, which sold the original Levi's. I worked there for quite some time. It was great – loads of bands used to come in. Sometimes I'd stay in London, because my girlfriend Suzanna lived in Wembley and it was easy to get to Hampstead from there.

RICH: It was all right for you. I was still stuck in East Grinstead, except for a dreadful job I got as a fire extinguisher salesman. The boss told me, 'There's this one salesman who is really good. I'll tell you what he does. He's got a herringbone jacket, and before he goes into a shop, he sprays it with lighter fuel. He sets it alight, runs into the shop shouting "Fire! Fire!" and pulls out the fire extinguisher and puts the fire out. That's how he makes his sales.' I said, 'I'm not doing that.'

FRED: Fucking hell.

RICH: I had to get out of East Grinstead, come hell or high water. I just remember thinking, 'How the fuck am I going to get a blowjob around here?'

I'm Too Sexy

Fairbrass/Fairbrass/Manzoli (1991)

Reprinted with permission from Spirit Music Group

I'm too sexy for my love, too sexy for my love
Love's going to leave me

I'm too sexy for my shirt, too sexy for my shirt, so sexy it hurts
And I'm too sexy for Milan, too sexy for Milan, New York and Japan
And I'm too sexy for your party, too sexy for your party
No way I'm disco dancing

I'm a model, you know what I mean
And I do my little turn on the catwalk
Yeah, on the catwalk, on the catwalk, yeah, I do my little turn on the
catwalk

I'm too sexy for my car, too sexy for my car
Too sexy by far
And I'm too sexy for my hat, too sexy for my hat
What d'you think about that?

I'm a model, you know what I mean
And I do my little turn on the catwalk
Yeah, on the catwalk, on the catwalk, yeah, I shake my little tush on the
catwalk

Too sexy for my, too sexy for my, too sexy for my

Cos I'm a model, you know what I mean
And I do my little turn on the catwalk
Yeah, on the catwalk, yeah, on the catwalk, yeah
I shake my little tush on the catwalk

I'm too sexy for my cat, too sexy for my cat
Poor pussy, poor pussy cat
I'm too sexy for my love, too sexy for my love
Love's going to leave me
And I'm too sexy for this song

RICH: The theme of irony runs through a lot of our songs – essentially, taking the piss – and 'Sexy' was all about that.

FRED: The idea of being too sexy for your shirt is gloriously ridiculous.

RICH: If we'd been completely gorgeous in 1991, it wouldn't have been as funny. People would think we were taking it seriously, but when you're a bald-headed bloke with muscles, and you're in your thirties, it's plainly ludicrous.

FRED: Funnily enough, it wasn't our idea to take our shirts off in the video. It was James Lebon, the video director. He said, 'Look how you're built. You can't have a song about being too sexy and not take your shirts off.' So we went with it.

Chapter 2

The Beautiful People

Crossing paths with Suicide, Joy Division, David Bowie, Mick Jagger and Bob Dylan... and that was before we were famous.

FRED: Our first band was called The Actors, when we were still living in East Grinstead, and we were active between 1977 and 1980. We had a couple of managers over the years. The first one was Roger Gray, who we knew because he owned a couple of record shops, and I worked for him. He didn't understand the business any more than we did, but nonetheless, he put the money in and had loads of enthusiasm. We got lucky with Roger – he had our backs through thick and thin during those early days.

RICH: We had a few different line-ups, but they tended to revolve around me on bass, you on acoustic and Mike Gerrard on guitar.

FRED: There were a couple of different drummers and we had a few lead vocalists. I'm not quite sure about this, but I think you were the first lead singer, and then we tried a Scottish guy called Jockey. After that it was a guy called Brian Howe, who went on to be quite successful in America with Bad Company. Brian was the best of all of us at the time. After him it was me, and then finally it was you again. I think that's right, anyway.

RICH: Yes, I think so. It's a long time ago. After Roger we had a manager called John Collins, who was managing Woody Woodmansey, who had played drums in David Bowie's Spiders

From Mars. Me taking over the vocals from Fred was John's idea, although I don't really know why I said yes. Back then, I'd never considered being a frontman.

FRED: I'm pleased you did, because I was shit.

RICH: As a band we worked hard in the early days. We did a gig at the Greyhound in Fulham once, and as we were playing, the sound was getting worse and worse, with more and more feedback, until it sounded really, really awful. Peering through the gloom, we saw that the soundman had fallen asleep on the desk, sliding all the faders up with his arms.

FRED: God, some of those early gigs were pretty dismal. Between about 1976 and maybe 1989, I think we played every music venue in London, except for the Brecknock in North London and the Red Cow in Hammersmith. All through the late seventies and most of the eighties we played the Nashville, the Orange, the Marquee, the 100 Club, the Rock Garden and the rest.

RICH: Back then nearly every London pub was a gig. It was fantastic. What bands do now, I have no idea. We were never interested in playing cover songs: we just wanted to write our own stuff.

FRED: When we were playing with a full band, we sounded good, though. For one thing, we had a proper drummer called Tommy O'Donnell. He was great…

TOMMY O'DONNELL: I first met Rich and Fred around 1977, when I was working in Shepherd's Bush for an instrument hire company. The job with the boys came either out of the *NME* or the *Melody Maker*. They gave me a tape of the stuff they were doing, and at the time their singer was Brian Howe, who had a really good voice.

FRED: We had a reputation for making what was called stream-of-consciousness pop, because we'd have this rambling kind of melody and lyrics over what was basically a pop song. I occasionally play some of the really old demos, and most of them are shit, but there's some good ideas here and there.

TOMMY: We had a rehearsal place on a farm in Crowhurst, just outside East Grinstead. It was owned by the sister-in-law of the famous jockey Bob Champion. Mr and Mrs Fairbrass rented out the top floor of Abbottswood to Brian and to Mike Gerrard, the guitar player. Fred organised all the money and we got stuck into the songs.

FRED: Mike was a really good guitarist, but we felt he didn't understand the game. He thought that being a great guitarist was enough.

TOMMY: Mike seemed to be the kingpin of the band, to me anyway. He would do the arranging and get the songs into some kind of shape, and it went from there. Unfortunately Brian wasn't pulling his weight. We'd be up there rehearsing, and he wouldn't get out of his bed on time. He'd roll up late. I don't think it was moving along fast enough for him. He was getting bored.

FRED: I wasn't surprised when Brian left and went to America and became very successful with Bad Company. After him, I became the singer; I was terrible at it. I can sing, but I was a shit frontman.

RICH: The problem was partly that you were impossibly rude to our audiences.

FRED: It's true – I was. I think I knew I wasn't very good, so I was defensive and insecure.

RICH: We were playing in Scotland once, and the audience didn't clap, so you said, 'Just because you didn't make it into the World Cup, don't take it out on us.'

FRED: Not a great way to endear yourself to the public. The crowd understandably got pissed off and became very hostile. We had to leg it.

RICH: You know, we tried to make that fucking band work for ten years. To be absolutely honest with you, I don't know why we kept on doing it that long. I was in my mid-thirties when we finally made it. Imagine that nowadays, with the charts full of 17-year-old singers.

FRED: Well, we did have some good songs, and we are impossibly stubborn.

RICH: True, I suppose. We had one song, which I still think is really good, called 'Terminal Love'.

FRED: That song was the first time I tried an Electric Mistress, which is a very famous modulation pedal by Electro-Harmonix. I turned it up full, and I loved it. But as a band, I think we sounded a bit confused. We never wanted to sound like the bands that we liked, because we were looking for an identity of our own. We always thought we would come up with it in the end, but it took us a very, very long time to do that.

RICH: You could say that. It took us ages to get our heads around how we wanted to sound. At one point, we were sounding like Bryan Adams, or one of those eighties rock bands with big hair. Ironically, we made it with no hair.

FRED: We really liked it at the time, though. I still like that kind of rock. It's fun, isn't it? You put the top down on your car and drive down the freeway.

RICH: I think we were looking for something a bit more unusual, although we didn't really know where we were going. There's an honest way of delivering vocals, but I hadn't realised that, because I was too busy trying to be other people.

FRED: We both were.

RICH: Because we've done so many shows, I'm very clear about who I am. We have an identity that feels very comfortable now.

FRED: When I listen to our old songs now, I feel there's a lack of personality. The music is very generic – that's what always bothered me.

RICH: When I look back, aside from sheer refusal to take no as an answer, I can't think of a reason why we persevered with the band, because I didn't know what we were trying to do, musically. Maybe it was just stubbornness.

FRED: Our managers liked us. That must have helped.

RICH: There is that. I know Roger Gray thought we were good. He thought we had something, because he could hear the occasional hook in the songs.

FRED: I think Roger was surprised at how much work was needed to make a band successful. I think he thought that his connections with the record retail business would make it easier.

RICH: Fortunately he liked you, and you worked in his shop. Nine times out of ten these things are driven by personal friendship.

FRED: He was definitely impressed by our work ethic. Although the band wasn't particularly good at the time, we were very, very determined. I was on the phone a lot and I was quite dogged about hustling for gigs.

RICH: Life was difficult, but we were driven by sheer bloody-mindedness, and a good thing too. There's hundreds of good bands out there that don't make it, even though they might be good enough. But most people don't persevere. That's all it is.

FRED: Our co-writer Joel asked us to make a list of the gigs we played in the really early days, and I came up with this one. This is all the venues in London which The Actors played in 1976 and 1977. Don't ask me to come up with exact dates, though, because I have no idea. We also played in Port Glasgow, Edinburgh, Liverpool, Bath, Romford, Hornchurch, Bognor Regis, and too many others to remember.

Egham Women's Institute
Ronnie Scott's, Frith Street

27

Windsor Castle, Harrow Road
The Kensington, Russell Square
Rock Garden, Covent Garden
Music Machine, Camden
The Green Man, Marylebone
The Orange, Fulham
The Greyhound, Fulham
The Nashville, Fulham
Hope and Anchor, Islington
The Clarendon, Hammersmith
Girls' Physical Education University, Essex
London School of Commerce
Monkberry's, Jermyn Street
The Cartoon, Croydon
The Alhambra, Brighton

RICH: Like most bands we had good nights and bad nights, but I suppose we were absolutely determined. It was a mountain that we had to climb.

FRED: Even a bad gig only takes one tiny thing to keep it going. If just one-tenth of a single song goes all right, that keeps you going to the next gig.

RICH: It got better for us, at least temporarily, in 1978, when we did a UK tour with Suicide, the American synth duo.

Survival Tip No. 2: Our First UK Tour

FRED: Yes, readers, you did read that correctly – we toured with Suicide. When we say our first tour was with that band, people usually look at us like we're completely mad. We played in Liverpool, London, Leeds, Manchester, Southampton and Edinburgh, mostly to punk crowds, because it was 1978.

FRED: One reason we got that tour was because we supplied the PA, we were the roadies and we were the support band. Buy one, get three.

RICH: To me, the tour felt like joining the army or something – meeting people that you'd never meet otherwise.

FRED: Suicide attracted a bonkers fucking crowd. We saw violence at the shows that you would never see anywhere else. The punks didn't give a flying fuck about the bouncers. We'd be backstage with Suicide, and members of the crowd would just walk into the dressing room and start bad-mouthing them.

RICH: That was the first time I ever saw anyone piss in a sink. I remember thinking, 'You dirty devil!'

FRED: While we were on stage at Eric's in Liverpool, somebody went into the dressing room and deliberately pissed on our clothes. Nice.

RICH: I went back to the dressing room and, not realising this, I put my jeans on, only to find they were soaking.

FRED: It didn't stop there – at another gig someone threw piss at us. They literally pissed into a glass and then threw it at the band. Punks were big on piss.

RICH: Suicide's singer Alan Vega later said that when he was on stage in Glasgow, someone threw an axe at his head. Holy fucking moly!

FRED: We were in a rehearsal studio after Public Image Limited had been in there, and they'd pissed in plastic bags and pinned them to the wall as some kind of statement. On the subject of bodily waste, after a show in Preston in 1991 we jumped into our hire car. It was pissing down, so I turned the windscreen wipers on, but they were stopped by an unidentifiable mass. I went out to investigate, and found that it was a pair of men's pants, full of fresh shit. We took some comfort from the fact that the car was a hire car – so no one knew it was ours.

29

RICH: That's such a happy memory... There was a lot of fighting in the audiences back then.

FRED: Oh yes. When we used to play the Windsor Castle in Harrow Road, the crowds were often rowdy. One night, they were throwing snooker balls at each other. That was one of many rites of passage.

RICH: Suicide themselves were very friendly, weren't they? I remember a few times when promoters refused to pay us, Alan Vega and Martin Rev stood up for us, and we got our money.

TOMMY: Alan Vega bought us a drink or two as we went along. He was just a regular nice bloke, although I know some people have difficulty believing that.

RICH: We spoke to Suicide quite a lot. They were supportive. There was one night when we didn't have a hotel room, and they put their foot down and got us one. I remember Alan Vega being quite chatty, and I also remember them drinking Bacardi. They were nice, although we were from very different worlds. We're from Sussex and they were raised in New York.

FRED: I saw a different side of life on that tour, some of which I liked. I enjoyed the anarchy and the idea of living outside the box, which we saw a lot of.

RICH: At a gig at the Kensington in west London, one guy had 'Love' and 'Hate' tattooed on his knuckles, and he came up to me after the show and whispered in my ear, 'I've got a bucketload of spunk for you.' So I legged it out the back.

FRED: A wise move.

RICH: At the Factory in Manchester on 28 July 1978, Joy Division played between us and Suicide.

FRED: I liked their singer, Ian Curtis: we chatted backstage for quite a while. A window was open, I think, and he mentioned that he was cold. I was wearing a sweatshirt over a long-sleeved jumper, so I said, 'You can have this,' and gave him my sweatshirt. He gave me his white short-sleeve shirt in return. That was a nice gesture. Less than a year later, he was dead.

RICH: Very sad.

FRED: It really was, and also quite shocking. When I heard about that, I was surprised to hear that he'd had problems with depression, because he showed no sign of that when I spoke to him. He was quite chatty and sociable, and we hit it off. Nowadays, having suffered from depression myself, maybe I would have spotted the symptoms.

RICH: That tour was the big turning-point for me. It was a wake-up call, because it taught us that we needed to up our game.

FRED: We also learned that if you want something to work, you have to work hard for it. We had no roadies, so we had to take care of all the equipment. Every night, we loaded it into the venue and set it all up, then we did our show, broke down the equipment, loaded it back in the van and drove off.

RICH: Suicide got a good deal from us. We supplied the PA system; we were the roadies and the support band. We had it all!

FRED: The Actors were pretty much over by 1980. We'd done that tour with Suicide, but otherwise it was just standalone gigs here and there. We weren't getting anywhere, and I think we began to wonder if maybe we'd just got it wrong. The truth is that we just couldn't bring ourselves to stop.

TOMMY: Mike Gerrard eventually handed in his notice, but in a very unusual manner. Apparently he moved in upstairs with a girl, and never came back down. Then he joined another band.

FRED: That's more or less what happened. There was a band living upstairs on the top floor, and I think Mike thought he had a better chance of success with them than with us, so he started popping upstairs and jamming with them. I don't remember us falling out with him or anything. I think we just stopped seeing him and it fell apart, like bands do, for no real reason.

TOMMY: I left before Mike did. There was a point where John Collins was getting a deal for us, but I got a call from Mike, who said, 'They have a record company interested, but they have misgivings about the drummer.' I didn't want to get in the way of the band, so I said, 'Fair enough. I'll go and do something else.'

RICH: Tommy is a good guy and a friend to this day. He taught us to stand our ground.

FRED: Tommy was great. He had been raised in Glasgow, and he didn't suffer fools gladly. When we weren't getting paid at a student union gig one time, he went to the student union office the next morning, grabbed a state-of-the-art golf ball typewriter and held it out of the window, threatening to drop it. Funnily enough, we got our money double-quick. He was a good guy to have around.

RICH: I suppose we left it so long to leave home because Mum and Dad were really supportive, so we didn't feel the need to move out. When we finally left in 1981, I was 28 and you were 25, which I know is late, but they were very generous with letting musicians crash in the house, so things like that were never an issue. You could actually argue that them being so generous had a negative effect on us, because if we'd left home sooner it might have given us more drive to succeed.

FRED: Mind you, between gigs and our jobs we weren't at home much. We still worked hard to make the band work, though. It took well over ten years to make it – not everyone would be prepared to do that.

RICH: True. As we said, East Grinstead had started to feel pretty dull. London was much more exciting, although the downside was that we had to do a load of awful jobs. Initially we had painting and decorating jobs just north of King's Cross. We worked in shops, restaurants, factories and bars, anything to keep us going.

FRED: I was a minicab driver for about two years, which was useful because I ended up selling amphetamines from my cab. I worked nights, because the party crowd and hookers were more than happy to buy my drugs. That paid my way very nicely. Although I was driving around with grammes of speed on me, London felt quite anarchic back then, so it didn't cross my mind that it was illegal.

RICH: What could possibly have gone wrong?

FRED: Well, fortunately I was never robbed or busted. At one point, though, I owed someone a lot of money, so I paid some acquaintances to take my car, a Ford Cortina, and set it on fire for the insurance money. It fucking worked too, and I paid off what I owed. That story probably sounds like bullshit, but there you go. It's indicative of the lifestyle we were leading at the time.

RICH: It really is. London was rough then, but at least it was fun. It's become unbearable, because it's been completely ruined by people's obsession with money and control. I have a real problem with people who want to control things, because that normally kicks the life out of it. The reason London was so vibrant back then was because there wasn't much control there. The same goes for New York: the reason that city is dead now is because there's too much control. From an artistic point of view, you absolutely have to have an element of chaos, otherwise creativity doesn't flourish.

FRED: As well as my minicab dealings, I also worked on pop music videos as a runner and assistant director. Teresa, my girlfriend at the time, introduced me to a bunch of different people – choreographers, dancers, directors and so on – and so I did all the early Five Star videos, as well as working with Womack & Womack, Billy Ocean and A Flock of Seagulls. I even did a video with a band called Willie and the Poor Boys, which was a project set up by Bill Wyman of the Rolling Stones. Ringo Starr, Jimmy Page, Paul Rodgers and Charlie Watts were in that band.

RICH: What does an assistant director do, anyway?

FRED: I don't really know – but I know what I did. I was somewhere between the cameraman and the director. I was communicating the director's orders to the crew and the actors, so I'd be the guy who says, 'Everybody shut up on the set!', or 'Take a twenty-minute break, and don't go far!' Or I'd sort them out with drugs: it was much cheaper to give the crew a couple of lines of coke so that they'd work late, rather than get a new crew in to work overnight.

RICH: Sounds glamorous.

FRED: It really isn't. I was basically a runner, and it was a very sporadic gig. I only did maybe three or four a year. Some of it was a lot of fun: one of the Five Star girls had a crush on me and kept bringing me cookies.

RICH: Did you get involved with her?

FRED: Good Lord, no, but I did like her cookies. I also did pre-production on 'A Kind of Magic' by Queen, and I did the video for 'Don't Leave Me This Way' with The Communards in some old warehouse. To be honest, some of those videos were a lot of fun.

RICH: While all this was going on, we were still playing gigs as Peaches and then In The Flesh, and trying to get the band signed. We came really, really close to a deal on a number of occasions. Close, but no cigar.

FRED: I remember one label called Electric Records in Margaret Street, London, whose head of A&R wanted to sign us but then became really ill.

RICH: I watched a Twisted Sister documentary recently, and in the film they said that anyone who wanted to sign them either became ill or was in a car crash. That rang a bell, because stuff like that kept happening to us.

FRED: The 'stream-of-consciousness pop' thing that we were doing interested a few labels, and we got a couple of development deals. We ended up in the studio with the intention of being produced by Rupert Hine, a well-known guy at the time, but he got involved in another project, so we had some other producer in whose name I can't remember. My point is that if we'd been totally ignored by everybody, we would have thought, 'What's the point?' – but we had some quite well-known people sniffing around.

RICH: This is probably why we kept on persevering for all those years.

FRED: Then there was the guy who signed The Cure, Chris Parry. He'd started Fiction Records, and he was interested, but then The Cure took off and that was his focus from then on. The same happened with Ensign Records, who signed The Boomtown Rats. They were really interested – but then the Rats broke.

RICH: Bloody hell. All these names remind me that, actually, we weren't a bad band, were we?

FRED: Exactly. I remember talking to a company called Bright Music, and this story is funny because it shows that we were starting to get more confident about who we were. Their guy set up a meeting at their office, so I waited for him in reception, but he wasn't there. After twenty-five minutes I walked out, and I met him on the way in. He said, 'I'm really sorry I'm late,' but I replied, 'I'm not coming to the meeting. If you can't make time for me now, you won't make time later on, so forget it,' and I left. A few years later, I bumped into him after we'd got massive. He came up to me and he said, 'You were absolutely right.'

RICH: What about that woman who worked for that US record company? She tried to sleep with us on many occasions, and we suspect that a deal would have been in the offing if we'd said yes.

FRED: I can't say I blame her. But I think that's what kept us going – these moments.

RICH: When we were doing research for this book, we dug out our old demos, and actually there's some pretty good songs in there.

FRED: I liked a track called 'Physical Boy'. That was the first song that you sang low on, or at least lower than usual. We'd developed a Billy Idol sort of sound, with that kind of pulsing beat that he had on 'White Wedding' and 'Rebel Yell'. 'Physical Boy' wasn't a bad song. It had a hook to it. We also wrote a track called 'Katie's Favourite Song' and a couple of other songs that weren't bad.

RICH: We should have been signed on those songs. Why weren't we?

FRED: Fuck knows.

RICH: We've never fitted in – I think that's made us single-minded.

FRED: We weren't totally arrogant, we just knew what we were capable of. Anyway, we still had some great opportunities in the eighties. Are you going to tell the readers about David Bowie?

RICH: Do you think I should?

FRED: Fuck yes!

RICH: All right then. I appeared in three of his videos: a long-form film called 'Jazzin' for Blue Jean' in 1984, 'Loving the Alien' in '85 and 'Underground' in '86. I was hired mainly because I was incredibly pretty.

FRED: Of course you were, love!

RICH: I got the initial interview through your girlfriend Teresa, who was a choreographer. Back in those days, every video that was made had to have dancers in it, although I was required to mime playing bass rather than actually dance. So I walked into the studio in D'Arblay Street, Soho, and looked around, but I didn't realise Bowie was in the room. I didn't clock him at first because he was sitting tucked away in the corner.

FRED: It was quite good money, wasn't it?

RICH: It was £300 for a day's work, which was more than I'd ever imagined. We said hello and he said, 'If you want this job, you'll have to cut your ponytail off.' I said, 'I'll cut anything off to get this job,' and he laughed. He was very approachable and didn't play the star role at all. In fact, he struck me as a little bit shy.

FRED: Were you starstruck?

RICH: No, I wasn't, but I was excited. I just thought it would be fun. It never crossed my mind about getting my foot in the door and all that kind of stuff.

FRED: And was it fun?

Survival Tip No. 3: Learning from the Best

RICH: It was fun and interesting, although it wasn't always comfortable: my part in 'Underground' was shot in one of these freezer units where you can see your breath because it's fucking freezing. I didn't know how videos at that level were made, you know, so that was a learning curve. I had to learn the parts on the bass, even though I was only miming them, because Bowie was quite particular about the bass parts. I had to mime them exactly as they were on the recordings, so they sent me the parts and I practised them for several days until I had all the little licks down.

FRED: We did a few things like that, I remember.

RICH: Yes, I was in a Boy George video too. We used to make extra money by doing that kind of thing.

FRED: Later, he was rude about 'I'm Too Sexy'. We didn't care, though, because the song was already breaking. The feeling was mutual.

RICH: Do you remember when we auditioned to be Holly Johnson's backing singers?

FRED: Did we? Why the fuck did we do that?

RICH: Well, Holly Johnson was a big name. It was in December 1988, very soon after Dad died, which we'll talk about later in the book. I remember going into a TV studio to do the audition, where we presumably sang a song. We just used to throw crap at the wall and see what stuck, so to speak. I do remember that at one audition there was a woman who played a tape to sing along to. She came in about a beat too late. Instead of apologising and starting again, she just kept singing, which meant that sometimes she was in tune with the music and sometimes she wasn't. It was completely ridiculous.

FRED: And then we worked with Mick Jagger in 1985. That was around the time we were playing regularly at Dingwalls in Camden Lock. I remember Dzal Martin was on guitar and Ray Weston was on drums: he later joined Iron Butterfly.

RICH: The Jagger gig means that we worked with both halves of the 'Dancing in the Street' duo. Go on, you can tell this story.

FRED: We both appeared with Jagger in a film that he was starring in called *Running Out of Luck*. We were playing members of his band, in a scene at the very end where he's rehearsing in a small room upstairs in a pub.

RICH: How on earth did we get called in to do that one?

FRED: Jagger used us because you'd done David Bowie and because he knew the director, Julien Temple. We met him at Nomis Studios, and he walked in with a six-pack of beer.

Like Bowie, he was friendly and communicative. He was great compared to a lot of artists we've met, who are 24-carat cunts, thinking how famous they are.

RICH: I couldn't agree more.

FRED: We had a drummer playing with us in the scene we shot, although I can't remember his name. I played guitar and you played bass. We ran through the track for two or three hours, and Jagger said, 'I want to be physical during this, so I'm going to come up and hit one of you.' He pushed you so hard that you hit the wall. For a small dude, he packed a punch.

RICH: He made it sound like it was going to be a slight tap, but it bloody wasn't.

FRED: Maybe he just wanted to hit you. You are very hittable.

RICH: He wouldn't be the first. That was all shot in a pub in London. I remember being at the pub, and we were upstairs, and we could hear 'Raspberry Beret' by Prince. That's quite a psychedelic song, and Jagger said, 'I didn't like the first incarnation of psychedelia,' which we assumed meant The Beatles. I remember that quite well.

FRED: For the actual shoot, we were pretending to be his band, hanging out in the dressing room. I remember the actor Jim Broadbent came in with a briefcase of money. He fell and the money went everywhere.

RICH: I had to kiss a ginger-haired girl down by the Thames in Jagger's 'Lucky in Love' video. We had to do multiple takes, so we were kissing for quite a long time. She was pretty buxom, as I remember.

FRED: So that was that. And then, out of the blue in 1986, we were asked if we wanted to work with Bob Dylan, who was looking for band members to act and perform in a film he was doing called *Hearts of Fire*.

RICH: Acting wasn't really at the top of our to-do list, was it?

FRED: 'Acting' is quite an elaborate word for what we were doing. What happened was that we got asked to do a photoshoot with Rupert Everett, the actor. The brief for the shoot was that he had to look like he was in a band, so we dressed up in goth clothes and posed, trying to look mean.

RICH: Rupert said to us, 'I'm doing a movie called *Hearts of Fire* with Bob Dylan and they need musicians for Bob's band. Is it something that might interest you?'

FRED: He said, 'They need a bass player and a guitar player. Let me put your names forward,' which was good of him. The casting people came back to us and said, 'The bass player is a speaking role, so Rich will need to be an Equity member.' Neither of us were Equity members, so the actor Mark Rylance got the gig as the bassist. I didn't need to speak, so I got the guitarist's part.

RICH: I was disappointed but not crestfallen – it would have been nice to meet Bob Dylan.

FRED: The director was Richard Marquand, who had directed *Return of the Jedi*, and the script was by Joe Eszterhas, who was very hot at the time because he'd written *Jagged Edge*, which Marquand also directed. So on paper, *Hearts of Fire* seemed quite promising.

RICH: The first scenes were shot in London, weren't they?

FRED: Yes, we did one or two days at Heaven, the London club, and then we fucked off to Canada. A lot of the gig was just miming, but they wanted us to be real musicians because if push came to shove and there was a problem of some kind, we would be able to plug in and play for real. That did happen a couple of times, although Mark Rylance couldn't play bass so we had to sort the bass-lines out.

RICH: It was a pretty high-calibre band, if I remember rightly.

FRED: It really was. We had Timmy Cappello on sax from Tina Turner's band, and Reb Beach, who is now in Whitesnake, played guitar and bass. I was on second guitar.

RICH: And Bob Dylan was playing the guitar and singing?

FRED: Oh yes, he was there too... Anyway, we flew to Hamilton in Canada, where we filmed at a place called the Copps Coliseum, which seemed huge to me at the time. I couldn't imagine playing a place like that, although we've actually played much bigger places since then. I think it was probably about the size of Wembley Arena.

RICH: Did you actually play live at any point?

FRED: Yes, occasionally we plugged in and played a few blues tracks – nothing memorable. What happened was that we all went to a couple of shows by a rock band called Halloween, who were big at the time in Canada. We got on stage before their show and used their audience for live shots – it seemed to me they were trying to get a live audience for fuck-all. They'd pay some extras down the front to do what they were told, and we did a short piece with John Candy, who rocked up and did a very short piece to camera. He was shouting something from the audience, like a heckler. The rest of the audience were probably thinking, 'What the fuck is going on?'

RICH: Which was what most people asked themselves when they saw the film.

FRED: Oh, definitely. *Hearts of Fire* is truly appalling. It's one of the worst-reviewed films ever.

RICH: What is it actually about?

FRED: The storyline is that an up-and-coming artist, Molly, played by a singer called Fiona Flanagan, meets Billy, Bob Dylan's character. While she's in England with Billy, she meets another artist, James Colt, played by Rupert Everett, and so the love tryst begins.

41

RICH: What was Dylan like?

FRED: He was quite friendly backstage; he seemed happy to chat with people. We were told to make an effort to interact with him, because apparently he isn't very good at going up to people and saying hello. We were told, 'He'll probably just stand there, so you have to go up to him and interact.' I don't think many people did that, though, because they felt a bit awkward.

RICH: Was there much going on behind the scenes, or was it all family-friendly?

FRED: I remember being in a backing singer's hotel room and the phone rang, and it was her fiancé. She started wanking off one of the musicians while she was talking to the guy on the phone, which was a bit surreal. I think she tried to cop off with Rupert Everett as well.

RICH: That's multi-tasking for you.

FRED: Otherwise, not much was happening. We were in Toronto at one point, and I had a few days off with nothing to do. The rest of the band were New York-based, so they were in and out, doing shows. We would shoot from Monday to Wednesday or whatever, and then they'd fuck off for four days. Mark Rylance and I were left to sit around with nothing to do but go on set.

RICH: It sounds a bit tedious.

FRED: It was at times, but it turned out that Dylan stayed pretty much on set the whole time we were there, and I got invited to his trailer to teach him the songs. He hadn't written all the songs for the film: there was a producer called Beau Hill who did that.

RICH: How come you had to go and teach him the songs?

FRED: He didn't know the chords to some of them, and he wanted to look as if he was playing the songs correctly, because the director wanted us to look like we were all on the same page. There were no other musicians around to go to Dylan's hotel room or his trailer, because they'd all gone to New York to play gigs, so they asked me, 'Would you go to Bob's trailer and run through a couple of songs before tomorrow's shoot?'

RICH: Why didn't Dylan just learn the songs by listening to them and figuring them out, like we have to?

FRED: Don't ask me. Anyway, I went over to his trailer with my guitar, I knocked on the door and he let me in. It was all very friendly. He had a couple of girls in there – Latino-looking, if I remember – who were drinking rum and rolling up these really big spliffs.

RICH: You asked me this question about David Bowie: were you starstruck?

FRED: And also like you with Bowie, no, I wasn't. I felt quite comfortable playing with him. I remember the songs were in F, B flat and C, which I played for him on my Telecaster, unplugged. He just said, 'What do we do here?' and I said, 'It goes to a relative minor at the bridge,' or whatever.

RICH: So it went smoothly?

FRED: Mostly, yes, although one time he had locking nuts on his guitar, and he'd never seen those before. He was trying to tune his guitar, but obviously the tuning wasn't going up and down because the locking nuts were locked onto the strings. I said, 'It doesn't work like that, Bob. These are called locking nuts.' And he said, 'What do you mean? Is it locked off here?' I guess he was obviously more used to vintage guitars.

RICH: Was he into the movie?

FRED: I think so, but then again, there was a song called 'The Usual' which we played on stage, although not in front of an audience. The band were on stage, just to make up the numbers, but really, it was all about Dylan singing into the camera. He started playing and singing the song, and the director asked him if there was a lyric sheet. Dylan said, 'It's okay, I'm just making Dylan sounds.'

RICH: Oh, that's great.

FRED: Isn't it? I don't really think he was born to be an actor. At one point he had to act a scene where he was smashing up a hotel room – apparently it took him nine days to do it. This was great for me, because the film got delayed so I got paid more.

RICH: Well, that was useful, because you and I had arranged to visit New York after your shoot finished, paid for by the *Hearts of Fire* gig.

FRED: It really was. The other thing that put the film back is that one of the main actors ordered vegetarian food on set, but they got his order wrong, so he smashed up his trailer.

RICH: What did you think of the finished film?

FRED: I went to the premiere in London, and it was embarrassing. Rupert Everett was practically hiding under his fucking chair. I think everybody already knew that the film was rubbish. I felt sorry for Richard Marquand, because he died shortly afterwards, so his career ended with a disappointing film. In America, it only came out for a week.

RICH: I've never seen it.

FRED: Don't bother. Anyway, I got paid, put it in the bank and flew in from Toronto just as you flew into New York. This was early November 1986.

RICH: We stayed there for about ten days.

FRED: Just enough to get a little taste for it. We really liked it there, and that made us decide to come back for a longer trip as soon as we could.

RICH: We were in touch with a guy in America who said he really liked what we did, and he asked, 'Have you heard of the

New Music Seminar?' We'd heard of it, but we didn't really know what it was. He said, 'You should come over to New York. I think it'd be interesting for you.' So we planned to go over again the following summer.

FRED: I did a moonlight flit from my flat in London, because I wanted to use my rent money for the New York trip. My landlord was a complete prick so I didn't feel bad about it.

RICH: We wanted the band to do well, and we'd been trying and failing to do that in London for years, so New York seemed like a good option.

FRED: We were fans of the early seventies New York music scene – Velvet Underground, Ramones, Blondie and Television – but what we didn't know was back in the sixties there was virtually nowhere in New York where you could play original music, just a couple of bars. CBGBs was there, but it was a shithole. They literally had a single lightbulb above the stage. We went there and spoke to the owner, Hilly Kristal, although we never played there for some reason.

RICH: It was really interesting to us how so much music came from this little pocket of the Lower East Side, all from about three blocks. Music sometimes seems to come out of these little areas, whether it's Manchester or Birmingham or Seattle. Not even entire cities, just certain districts.

FRED: Moving to London had opened up the floodgates for us, in that we saw the way that different way people lived. When we went to New York in '87, it was even better: you felt able to do things that you couldn't possibly do at home, because of the repercussions that might come back to your doorstep. We took full advantage, didn't we?

RICH: Oh yes. This is where it all started to get very weird.

Do Ya Feel

Fairbrass/Fairbrass/Manzoli (1991)
Reprinted with permission from Spirit Music Group

Jean speaks French, not a word is said
For those who set sail on her water bed
It's a fetish cruise, our pleasure to
Do business with you
Do ya feel like taking 'em down
Do ya feel like taking 'em down

Now love and hope, trust and faith
After prayer it's back to Alice's place
Peaches and cream, angel food
If you can't get up then just get rude
Do ya feel like taking 'em down
Do ya feel like taking 'em down
Do ya feel like taking 'em down
Do ya feel like taking 'em down

Fight it all you want, it's a love machine

Jean's well aware, that time's no friend
Gravity's calling, the party will end
But until it does, love's for lunch
Half the world blows and
Half the world sucks

Do ya feel like taking 'em down
Do ya feel like taking 'em down
Do ya feel like taking 'em down
Do ya feel like taking 'em down

Fight it all you want, it's a love machine

RICH: I love singing this song live because it goes down really well. It's got a very slinky shuffle pattern that changes over two chords. The bass is very cool. We've only ever found one bass player apart from Phil Spalding who could get it as slick.

FRED: This is a song about a fading prostitute, and one of my favourite lines is 'Jean speaks French, not a word is said / For those who set sail on her water bed'.

RICH: We used the idea of setting sail in 'Deeply Dippy' as well. We're very big on sailing!

FRED: I like the line about 'Half the world blows and half the world sucks'.

RICH: I remember driving down to Basingstoke to see Stuart, and you had sent me the work-in-progress drums for this track, so I was listening to them in the car. They sounded rubbish at the time, but obviously I didn't know what the fuck I was talking about, because they sound great now.

Chapter 3

On the Way Up

Fame, fortune and falling into the belly of the beast.

FRED: We loved New York. For some reason, it really suited us, so we went back there in May 1987. There was an interesting start to our first day in NYC. We were asleep on the floor of our apartment, and one of the hookers we lived with, Joan, crouched naked just inches above your face. She woke you up with the words, 'I've just shaved my pussy. Do you like it?'

RICH: The goal was to get ourselves some gigs and see if we could attract some attention. Over the five or six months we were there, we achieved that goal, we were featured in the New York Seminar, we got great reviews and Capitol/EMI signed us on a development deal.

FRED: I remember we played all over Manhattan, including the Knitting Factory, the Shark Club, bars on Bleecker Street and even at an Indian restaurant in Times Square that morphed into a gig at night. We plugged our Walkman into the PA system, while I played live guitar over it, Rich sang lead and my ex, Teresa, sang backing vocals. The other bands brought a huge amount of equipment. They looked at us like we were cunts.

RICH: It was a taste of freedom, in a way. When you're in a different place, especially a foreign place, you have no friends or anybody that can tell you what's right or wrong or good or bad. You're completely free to make your own way.

FRED: That made New York perfect for us.

Survival Tip No. 4: Be Fearless

RICH: There was a really experimental atmosphere over there at the time. It was vibrant. I firmly believe that you have to take the brakes off to let things happen. If you do what the fucking politicians want you to do all the time, which is control you, you kill it stone-dead.

FRED: Other lessons that we learned in New York came from elsewhere, though, with the jobs we did and the people we met.

RICH: We stressed about money at first, but it was fine once we both got jobs. I worked in a gay gym, or a gym that was about 70 per cent gay anyway. I was put on the phones because they thought I sounded posh. It was a basement gym on Sixth Avenue, and I really enjoyed it. When I was on the phone and new members came in, I had to tell them that there were lots of gay guys here, and if that was a problem for them, then they probably shouldn't train here. One Wall Street guy definitely had a problem with the gay clientele – he was chased off the property for being abusive and legged it down Sixth Avenue with his briefcase flapping in the wind.

FRED: That was when we first got serious about fitness training: we'd been toying with the idea for a while.

RICH: What I liked about New York was feeling that I lived there. I wasn't a tourist. I'd go down to a corner shop every morning and get milk for the gym – the kind of everyday task that you do when you actually live in a place.

FRED: I mostly worked in restaurants and bars. They were all left of centre and slightly underground. I felt quite at home in those places, because I liked stuff that was slightly off the radar. One of them was the Art Cafe on Astor Place, off Second Avenue. I was a busboy, which means that you just tidy up tables and deliver water, you don't take orders. I sometimes made $200 a night at weekends, which was good money back then. It was a really busy restaurant, with loads of people from the City, but they didn't like the traders who came in off Wall Street, so the barman used to put magic mushroom tea into the cocktails. By the end of the evening the traders were all hallucinating – he took great pleasure in watching them.

RICH: We lived with a friend for most of the time we were there. It was so weird because when we stayed with him six months before, he was as straight as a die and worked in theatre on Broadway. Wind forward six months and he'd turned into Scarface.

FRED: Every day, it was madness. There was coke everywhere: in the fridge, in the bathroom, in drawers, on the TV, literally everywhere you looked. Plus, there were lots of weird and wonderful people visiting every day. It reminded me of how Warhol's Factory might have been, but without the art. Our bedroom was a dump room full of bikes, old furniture and general crap with a mattress on the floor for us to sleep on. It was summertime and unbearably hot: there was no air-conditioning, just a huge industrial fan that was extremely noisy.

RICH: It was completely anarchic. New York was amazing back then, just before Giuliani and the big cleanup.

FRED: It was very hedonistic. We went to a lot of events and clubs – the Tunnel, Arena, the Saint, the Pyramid and the Limelight. You worked at Nell's and I got a job at Trash and Vaudeville, which is a very famous clothes shop. I met Vernon Reid of Living Colour and Billy Idol's guitarist Steve Stevens

51

there, because it was one of those rock'n'roll hangouts. It's still there. It's featured in *Seinfeld*.

RICH: In New York in those days, you were allowed to be almost anything you wanted to be. It was incredible, a chaotic place. I worked the door at Nell's Night Club on West 14th Street: my job was to count the boys and girls, keeping two to one in favour of the girls. I was also on toilet duty, monitoring the drug use and trying to make sure that only one person at a time went into the cubicles. The logic was that people usually like to snort coke together. On one occasion I saw two pairs of feet – one in stilettos, the other in City brogues – so I banged on the door and shouted, 'One of you will have to come out!' I assumed it was a man and a woman, but in fact the stilettos were worn by a little guy in a boob tube and tiny shorts. Those clubs were fantastic, with people losing their minds every weekend.

FRED: Did you cop off with anyone while we were in New York?

RICH: Not really. I met one guy, who invited me to his house in Hicksville. I ended up sleeping in his sister's bed. She wasn't in it, I should add.

FRED: Oh dear.

RICH: It didn't matter. I really liked New York. I used to walk home at about four in the morning, and as I walked up Sixth Avenue, everything was completely dark – but I never got any grief, ever. So I think the image of old New York as being hopelessly dangerous is partly postcode- and experience-driven.

FRED: We had a gig lined up at the Knitting Factory, so we arrived with our Walkman. Looking back, that approach was actually quite out there. It was quite punky, I suppose. It was a very novel way to perform back then, but we didn't realise it.

RICH: The gig at the Knitting Factory was the catalyst we needed. We received great reviews and that triggered the record labels to circle around us.

FRED: The next day, I was coming home from my nightshift at the Art Cafe, and I know this sounds like a scene from a movie, but on the pavement was a newspaper with our faces on it. I thought, 'What the fuck is that?' so I picked it up, and it said, 'The Brits are coming!', with this glowing review. It read: 'This band have no drummer and they're really anarchic' and so on. When we got back to the apartment where we were living, we were told, 'The phone's gone mad – the fucking world and his wife are on the answerphone.'

RICH: One of the messages was from June Honey, who worked for a promoter, and she recommended that we speak to a guy called Bennett Glotzer. We didn't know much about him at the time, but it turned out that he'd managed all these massive artists – Janis Joplin, Frank Zappa and Blood, Sweat & Tears among them. We also didn't know that he was reputedly a 'made man' with the American mafia, and therefore very influential for that reason.

FRED: Bennett said, 'You gotta come and meet me!', so we went to see him at a big fuck-off hotel Midtown. He said, 'Who do you want to be signed to?' And we said, 'What do you mean?' He said, 'Let's just ring a label and do a deal. I'll call the head of Capitol.' He calls Capitol and says, 'I got a band! Okay, good. Signed!' and slams the phone down. That was it. It was a $60,000 development deal, with the promise that we would record for Capitol when we got home.

Survival Tip No. 5: **It's All Bollocks Until It's in the Bank**

RICH: We only saw $2,000 from that development deal. We were fucking furious, and I drowned my sorrows with a bottle of Southern Comfort. Stuart came home and found me lying on the floor with the empty bottle. I was wondering where our $58,000 went.

FRED: We realised what was going on and went to see a lawyer. The moment we mentioned Bennett Glotzer's name, he said, 'Walk away and wait for the contract to expire – it's only a year.'

RICH: What was funny was that, apart from ripping us off, Bennett was a very nice guy, at least when he was with us. He was actually quite supportive. Two girlfriends of ours, Katie and Teresa, wanted to go on holiday in LA, so he said, 'They can come and stay at my house,' because he had this huge place in Beverly Hills. They told us later that when they were staying there, one night all the lights went on in the garden. They looked out and he was out in the backyard with two shotguns, shouting, 'I know you're fuckin' there!' He thought someone was in his garden.

FRED: Years later, I was talking to the manager of a well-known band, and he told me a story about Bennett Glotzer. The band were starting to do well in Italy, and a major promotion schedule was scheduled for them. They're waiting in their hotel room before going to the TV studio, and there's a knock on the door. Two guys walk in and one of them says, 'I'm really looking forward to doing business with you.' The manager says, 'Who are you?' but the guy won't answer, so he tells them to leave. They do, and two hours later, the booking agent calls and says, 'What's going on? Your TV appearances and shows have all been pulled.' The manager says, 'What the fuck is happening?' and rings the label back in the UK. The people in the UK speak to the label in America, who tell them, 'Well, you pissed off the wrong people.' He says, 'What do we do?' They tell him he's got to speak to Bennett Glotzer. So he rings him up; he agrees to help. An hour later, the TV appearance is back on. The manager said it was unbelievable. He said everything stopped within half an hour, and then everything was back on two hours later, after one call from Bennett.

RICH: Be careful who you piss off.

FRED: But this was how those old-time managers used to work. We used to know the former head of a major label, who told us stories about Peter Grant, who managed Led Zeppelin. He told us that even if Led Zeppelin were on holiday, and there was no album out, and they had nothing at all to promote, Peter Grant would ring the record company up every day and shout, 'What the fuck are you doing for my band?' He was like a rabid dog. His desire to hassle people wasn't determined by his band actually doing anything. As an artist, I think it would have been really good to have a manager like that. Someone who will go out to bat for you.

RICH: Sometimes you need to resort to those very primal tactics in this business, because people will take advantage of you if you don't. If you're polite and kind, they think you're soft.

FRED: We talked to Mike Krum, who was a very successful American radio plugger and promoter. He told us that back in the day, and I know it sounds ridiculous, his people would go into a radio station with new releases and show the DJ or the programme controller a briefcase. This case had three compartments – one with a gun, one with money and one with cocaine – and they would say, 'Take your pick'. He said, 'That's just what we did back then.' He certainly had the platinum discs and chart successes to back up his story.

RICH: We met quite a few unique people in New York. Our landlord introduced us to a porn star, Marc Stevens, whose nickname was '10½' for obvious reasons. He'd been a pioneer of the sex industry in the seventies, particularly in New York, and he'd been photographed by Robert Mapplethorpe. He asked us to do a porno movie with female twins.

FRED: The brief was that we would be having sex with the twins, in other words two brothers shagging two sisters. It would have been a day's work, or whatever. We went to his apartment opposite the Chrysler Building to discuss it, and he opened the door in nothing but a posing pouch, with his chest covered in glitter. He was very tanned and good-looking, and his apartment was covered in deep shag-pile carpet, with multiple TV sets everywhere playing porn to get us in the mood. That's when we got introduced to freebasing, which isn't that dissimilar to crack.

RICH: To be honest we were skint, so we thought about it for a second.

Survival Tip No. 6: **Big Cocks Aren't Everything**

FRED: Marc then took us into his bedroom and showed us a huge mirror cut into the carpet. He said to us, 'I'm going to teach you how to love your cock.'

RICH: Like we didn't already.

FRED: He took his dick out and we realised how he got his nickname, because this thing was fucking enormous. He started to stroke it and said, 'Now, Fred, take out your cock. You've got to learn to love your cock.' I said, 'After seeing yours, no fucking way!' Marc then stood astride the mirror and slowly massaged his penis. We think he wanted us to cherish our masculinity. We were so stoned, fuck knows what he was on about.

RICH: As we've already said, not all men are created equal.

FRED: He was going to pay us $1,500 each for one day, which was a lot of money for us in 1987, but we just couldn't face it.

RICH: As for the freebasing, it was really intense. I don't like taking anything that takes you out of your ability to control what you say and do.

FRED: It's very different to doing a line of coke. Your heart rate goes bonkers, and you feel great euphoria and a complete disconnection with your surroundings. It's slightly hallucinogenic too.

RICH: It's a head-to-toe experience, and after a massive spike in euphoria, you come down again.

FRED: We then went out onto Marc's terrace, overlooking the Chrysler Building, and I was so off my head on this stuff that I thought I could step right across Broadway onto the Chrysler Building. Luckily someone said that was a bad idea. Later, Teresa came and got us out of there, which was good because we were in a mess.

RICH: Looking back, Marc obviously had his demons, although he was a lovely guy. Life had treated him badly or maybe he made bad choices. For ten years he'd been male adult film actor of the year, and a celebrity. We learned later that he died in 1989.

FRED: It was fun in New York, but it was definitely dangerous. I remember walking down a street and hearing gunfire – a guy was shooting cars. I hid in a doorway and waited for him to go away.

RICH: It didn't matter. We really liked New York.

FRED: That said, we were shocked when our flatmate Chrissy was killed over a bad drug deal. We said one night, 'Where's Chrissy?' And they said, 'Chrissy got shot tonight,' almost in passing. She'd got involved with the wrong people, unfortunately.

RICH: I worked in a flea market for a couple of weeks during the summer: it was sweltering. What was interesting is that it felt incredibly familiar – quite European – but just a block down the street, there was a completely different feel. I liked the contrast.

FRED: I wish we could have stayed longer, but we thought we had to get home to start recording for Capitol Records – and we were running out of cash.

RICH: I had friends and family that I missed and wanted to see. The New York trip was incredibly good for us, though, because when we came back, it reignited our enthusiasm.

FRED: London seemed quite dull compared to New York, I remember.

RICH: It really was. When we came back to London and I went to Leicester Square on a Saturday evening, it was dead compared to what we'd experienced in New York. I remember thinking, 'It must be a Sunday or a Monday,' but it wasn't. We started working at the Dance Attic gym in Putney, London, right after we came back from New York. We worked there for the best part of four years until 'I'm Too Sexy' broke.

FRED: I really enjoyed working there, so I went and did an Amateur Bodybuilders Association course. I've still got my certificate somewhere. It's the minimum requirement if you want to train people in a gym, so it made sense. I was considering fitness as a career, and also I really enjoyed training. We changed our band name to Right Said Fred at this time. Our friend Katie Randall suggested it, having heard the Bernard Cribbins song of the same name.

RICH: At the time it didn't feel like a big deal. We changed our name every time we felt like it. If you had a couple of bad gigs with a particular name, we thought, 'Let's just get a new one.' I think Jethro Tull did the same thing in the early days.

FRED: We played some decent gigs in the three-year period between coming back from New York and releasing 'I'm Too Sexy'. We busked in Covent Garden, we played in a private members' bar called Fred's, we did the Mean Fiddler and Jongleurs in Clapham, the Chelsea Brasserie and a bunch of others.

RICH: We used to walk into restaurants and just start playing. We refused to play cover versions so it was always our own material.

FRED: We would just walk up the street, looking at restaurants, and say, 'That one will do.' At one of them, Braganza in Wardour Street, the guy came out and said, 'Come back and I'll book you,' so we started playing there regularly.

RICH: We just wanted to write and perform our own stuff. I think it's why we got thrown out of a few places. They probably wanted 'Volare' or 'La Bamba'. Although we knew we were being scouted by record labels, the acoustic thing ran its course.

FRED: We met Rob Manzoli in 1990 after we put an advert in a rehearsal room, the Ritz in Putney, where I worked on and off through the eighties. He was an interesting guitarist. I think he'd been playing with funk bands in Canada before we met him.

RICH: We had some really good laughs with Rob back in the early days. He had a good sense of humour.

FRED: Right after we met Rob, we were on Keith Chegwin's talent show, *Search for a Star*, but believe me, it wasn't intentional. We knew someone who knew someone who worked on the show, which we thought was just a regular music programme where artists just played songs. It turned out to be a competition, but we didn't know that, so we turned up, played our song and left as quickly as possible.

RICH: This was probably the last gasp for us, I'd say. We'd been trying to make it as a band since what – 1978? By the time we were working in the gym at Putney, it had been more than ten years since the Suicide tour, for Christ's sake.

FRED: Luckily, during one of our many 'What the fuck are we going to do?' chats, we had a meeting with our former manager Peter Gross. He said, 'I know I'm not your manager any more, but hear me out. You need to go to the top of the mountain and find your cutting edge.'

RICH: We thought, 'Cutting edge? What the fuck is he talking about?'

FRED: He then said, 'You need to find what you're about. Know thyself!', which made sense. We actually took that advice on board for a change. I had been made homeless shortly before this, so I was sofa-surfing at this point. Some soul-searching was very much needed.

RICH: Peter had been really good to us. He'd given us loads of gigs at his club, Dingwalls, and he'd helped us out with a few quid here and there, so we thought, 'He wouldn't say this unless he felt it.'

FRED: By this time, we were bored with the acoustic stuff. We thought, 'Why don't we listen to Peter and not be cunts for a change?' We went home and talked about what to do. I'd been going to nightclubs for some time by now, and was really into house music. I heard 'Pump Up the Volume' by MARRS, and I just thought, 'That is what we need to be doing – songs with bass right in people's fucking faces.'

RICH: We said to each other, 'Let's find another direction.'

FRED: The idea of doing danceable music was triggered by being in New York. We had heard a lot of club music there, and we liked it, so when we got back to London, we started going to a club called Reflex in Putney, and then another one called Double Bass in Earl's Court. I remember thinking that we should be making this kind of music, but with guitars.

RICH: Music was changing radically at the time. Programmers and DJs were front and centre, so we decided to try and shift our music away from the rock thing that we'd been doing for so long.

FRED: The tracks that struck us during the late eighties and early nineties were 'Ride on Time' by Black Box, '3 a.m. Eternal' by KLF and 'Groove Is in the Heart' by Deee-Lite.

RICH: I went to a few clubs when my partner Stuart was well, but when his health started deteriorating, it just wasn't possible, so we stayed in. I'm going to talk about Stuart a lot more later in the book, because he was the centre of my life for many, many years. For now, though, I'll just say that you were much more club-driven than I was, so Stuart and I used to stay at home a lot and watch endless episodes of *Star Trek*.

FRED: Meanwhile, I was going out to clubs nearly every night and thinking about the music I was hearing at the time – Technotronic, The B-52's' 'Love Shack', 'Express Yourself' by Madonna and 'Funky Cold Medina' by Tone-Lōc. I knew I wanted to play guitar on our songs, so I was going to have to figure out a way to do that.

RICH: In 1989, you shaved your head. Well, actually Stuart shaved your head. He said, 'You're losing your hair – just shave it off.' As it looked kind of cool, I did it too. It was a completely different look for us, especially as we were training hard and putting on muscle.

FRED: In 1990, we met a programmer and producer called Brian Pugsley and asked him to help us with a song that we had. It was really just your bass-line, which we'd already used on an earlier song called 'Heaven'. We'd never worked with a programmer before, but we wanted to work with someone who could do beats, and he'd been recommended to us. We went to his basement flat and he programmed up a drum and bass loop. It was just basic house music at that point.

RICH: I'd been sitting around for hours, so I went into Brian's bedroom, a bit stoned, just to stretch my legs. It had been a hot day, so I took my shirt off. I could hear the bass part coming from the other room, and while watching myself in the mirrors on his wardrobe door, I started singing this bizarre phrase out of the blue.

FRED: Which was?

RICH: As I recall, it was something to do with being too sexy for my shirt.

FRED: Was it really? And where did that come from?

RICH: I have no idea. I'm not in the habit of describing myself as sexy. It just popped into my head. God works in mysterious ways.

FRED: Thank the Lord. You and Rob loved it immediately, but I took some convincing.

RICH: Well, you were always a bit slow on the uptake.

FRED: After you came up with that line, I wrote the rest of the lyrics to 'I'm Too Sexy'. Everyone can relate to the lyrics about 'my cat' and 'What d'you think about that?', but I was also writing about our experiences in New York, where we'd witnessed the rise of the supermodel – plus I was dating a model at the time. She had actually said to me when we met, 'I'm a model, you know what I mean?'

RICH: The culture of the supermodel was huge at the time. We thought the idea of someone being so consumed by their own gorgeousness that they can't function was hilarious, and this song takes the piss out of that kind of person.

FRED: We specifically chose iconic place names and symbols, such as car, hat, cat, party, New York and so on, because we didn't want the lyric to date.

RICH: It's been implied by people that we were working in a gym and somebody brought this song to us, and we took our shirts off and that was it – but that was just the rumour mill.

FRED: We had a lot of fun writing 'I'm Too Sexy'; maybe because it was such a departure from where we'd been before, musically. We did the vocals in a studio in Ealing in west London. It was cold, dark and freezing.

RICH: It wasn't a great working environment. The studio had gone into receivership, but if you gave the caretaker some cash, he'd open it up at night, just as long as you didn't switch on any lights or put on the heating.

FRED: We had to work from the lights on the equipment and some little spotlights in the studio.

RICH: That was where I recorded the vocal that's on the final version.

FRED: What turned everything around was when we met Tamzin Aronowitz, who became our manager. She was the receptionist at a studio called Red Bus, and she offered to try and get us a deal. We told her we didn't care about a deal, we just wanted to hear it on the radio. We were sick of labels and their idiotic, cloth-eared A&R teams.

RICH: Tamzin was very young, maybe 18 years old, but she actually did what she said she was going to do, which was rare for our managers – in fact most managers, in our experience.

FRED: Once the vocals were recorded, Tamzin hooked us up with a programmer called Ian Craig Marsh, who had worked with Heaven 17. After that, we wanted to add some more beats, because we knew that we had to get more of a dance version of the song. Tamzin played the song for a plugging company called Gut Reaction, who liked it, but they said it needed to be a dance record. We initially approached the DJ Jeremy Healy, but he said no. However, he worked with a DJ and programmer called Tommy D, who we asked if he'd work on 'Sexy' with us. He later sent us a backing track which we liked.

RICH: Tamzin arranged studio time at Red Bus, where we finished 'I'm Too Sexy'. The bass was recorded by Phil Spalding. We were insistent that the bass followed the vocal line, and Phil added his own touches.

FRED: The track was finished at Red Bus Studios in January or February 1991.

RICH: We sent cassettes to every label we could think of. Oh my God, that was an experience.

FRED: They all hated it. The most aggressive and unpleasant reply was from Island Records. They said, 'Not only will no one ever buy this song, no one will ever buy an album with this song on it.' They hated the song with a vengeance.

FRED: In the end, Tamzin and Gut Reaction managed to get the 12-inch single version to Gary Crowley and the 7-inch version to Simon Bates. Simon had the morning breakfast show on BBC Radio 1. This was a defining moment for us, because Simon played it off the acetate, and the listener reaction was brilliant. Many thanks to Gary Crowley and Simon Bates for that leap of faith.

RICH: The record immediately went fucking bonkers.

FRED: It went stratospheric in a matter of days. Gut Reaction set up Tug Records to release the track. We still hadn't signed a record deal at this point.

RICH: Tug Records officially released the single on 12 July 1991. The minute it got onto radio, it started getting massive numbers. Suddenly people knew who we were. Soon after that, we shot a video with director James Lebon, as there was a demand for it.

FRED: Part of the reason we shot some of that video outdoors in Notting Hill Gate was because the studio generator packed up.

RICH: We stopped working at the gym because the demand for club appearances escalated. The money was very useful. We'd simply perform 'I'm Too Sexy' once or twice and then go on to the next venue.

FRED: 'Sexy' was so new and broke so quickly that we were getting to know the song at the same time as our audience.

RICH: It took a while for that to sink in.

FRED: Our first *Top of the Pops* appearance was in August 1991. It was quite a surreal experience. We'd been avid *Top of the Pops* fans since we were kids – and now we were on it.

RICH: I met David Bowie on that *Top of the Pops*. I was standing backstage, and he walked up to me and said, 'What are you doing here?' because I think he thought I was making tea or something. I told him we had a hit record and we both laughed. It was six years since I had worked on his videos.

FRED: Do you ever watch that first *Top of the Pops* appearance?

RICH: No. Who the fuck watches themselves anyway?

FRED: So now we had a UK hit. For overseas releases, we had a guy called Bob Cunningham at Total Records working on the song. He was the licensing agent, or whatever the correct term is. We think his first ports of call were Belgium, Holland and Scandinavia, all of which kicked off very nicely, and I think 'Sexy' was number one in Ireland too. Then it just started rolling out everywhere. If I remember rightly it ended up being number one in thirty-two countries, if you can believe that.

RICH: I can barely believe it myself.

FRED: On another note, it didn't take long for the stalkers to appear. Remember that woman who thought that you and she were married?

RICH: Oh God, yes. I started getting these love letters at the gym where we trained. She seemed to think that we were married, and she thought we'd done things together that we obviously hadn't done. She'd write, 'What a nice evening at the theatre we had the other evening,' or whatever. I asked our press people how I should respond, and they said, 'Don't respond at all.'

FRED: I would think responding is the worst thing you can do in that situation.

RICH: Yes, it would have been. She started sending more letters: the writing was very close together, and there were upside-down crosses on them. I ignored them, so this woman got really fucked off. First she sent me a Valentine's card torn in half, and then a rice pudding arrived at the gym. Obviously I didn't touch it – which was a good job, because it was full of broken glass.

FRED: We reported this to the police, but it got even worse: this woman accused you of taking money out of her account. Fortunately, it turned out that the police already had her on record as suffering from a serious mental illness.

Survival Tip No. 7: Be Careful Who You Trust

FRED: 'Don't Talk Just Kiss' was our second single, released in November 1991. It did very well, particularly in South America and the UK, and unexpectedly well in Germany. 'I'm Too Sexy' tanked first time around in Germany – so 'Don't Talk Just Kiss' being such a big hit there was fantastic.

RICH: At that point, we knew we'd buried the one-hit-wonder tag.

FRED: Someone working with us at the time tried to block the release of 'Don't Talk Just Kiss', claiming that they had written parts of it. It was all bollocks. Have a hit, get a writ.

RICH: Another game-changer was when 'I'm Too Sexy' broke into the US *Billboard* charts.

FRED: That song's success in the USA was partly due to an American DJ, who attended an event in Manchester called In the City in 1991. He couldn't get away from 'I'm Too Sexy' because it was all over British radio, so he bought a copy and took it back to the USA, where he had a drivetime show on a tastemaker station. In America, those stations rule the roost and influence other stations, so when he started playing 'Sexy', it suddenly started gaining momentum all through America, and a licensing deal with Charisma Records was agreed.

FRED: We were told we were number one in America when we were sitting in St Lucia airport, which at that time was very small. A phone on the wall was ringing and ringing. A member of the airport staff eventually picked it up and asked, 'Is Right Said Fred here?' Tamzin was handed the phone and it was Hit & Run, our publishers: they told us we were that week's number one in America.

RICH: The minute that happened, my partner Stuart started crying. He thought it meant that he would never see me again, because I'd have to go off and be famous. I was a touch pissed off, but that was how he was: I think it was a combination of jealousy and the fear of being left, in equal measure.

FRED: The first time we heard ourselves on US radio was in Miami, when we'd hired an open-top Thunderbird sports car. The radio DJ said, 'And this week's *Billboard* number one is Right Said Fred with "I'm Too Sexy".' That was an extraordinary moment.

RICH: I think that was the first moment I thought, 'Fuck! Who woulda thunk it!'

FRED: Damn straight. An independent band with no money, making it that big? You've got to be dreaming. Some bands only make it if they borrow a huge amount of money from a major label, but then they spend the next ten years trying to pay it off. Everything we made was profit, because we hadn't spent much money.

RICH: We didn't have any to spend!

FRED: We flew over to the USA for a six-week promo tour in the spring of 1992, on a very limited budget.

RICH: We were flying around America, going to local radio stations and playing in shopping malls. It was mental. Every day we'd get up, do a morning radio show, film morning TV, and then we'd jump on a plane to the next city. Once we'd landed we'd do press all afternoon, have a bite to eat and then do a show, before going to bed at one or two in the morning. Then it started all over again.

RICH: One of the most memorable gigs was in Austin, Texas. The parking lot was full of motorbikes, and our tour manager warned us that things could get rough. I was wearing a transparent white bodystocking, and I thought we were going to get murdered. The venue had chicken wire on a roll above the stage, like they had in *The Blues Brothers*, and they asked us if we wanted to unroll it in front of the stage. We said no. Fortunately, the audience loved us.

FRED: Seriously, the bikers thought we were great. They were very cool.

RICH: I remember we were walking out of a diner in Texas, and coming towards us across the car park were two massive bikers who had just got off their Harleys. They both dropped to their knees and said, 'We're not worthy!'

FRED: We hadn't seen *Wayne's World* yet, so we didn't know what they were on about.

RICH: The main thing was that they liked us. That was a relief.

Survival Tip No. 8: **Read the Small Print**

FRED: What we discovered much later was that one of the reasons shows were added to the end of a day of promotion was to enable the record label to offload 50 per cent of its promotion costs onto us. Technically, adding a show made that day a 'show day' – not just a promotion day.

RICH: The influence of 'Sexy' ran deep in America. Apparently 'I'm too sexy for school' was a popular excuse for truancy. A politician actually said, 'I can't comment on this, I'm too sexy.' In Texas, we heard there was a fight in a bar because some girls played the video for eight hours continuously, and when a guy tried to turn it off, they beat him up.

FRED: We were also told that a man died from what the coroner reported as 'oral asphyxiation'. The poor man requested 'I'm Too Sexy' at a lap dancing club and had a heart attack while the stripper was dancing.

RICH: As we understand it, she had huge breasts, and he buried his head between them while the song was going on and suffocated... Anyway, Madonna stated on TV that she wanted to have sex with me. I never actually met her, but she's obviously got good taste.

FRED: Would you have slept with her, if the opportunity had arisen?

RICH: I think so, yes. When that quote came out, I liked it because I thought she was quite sexy too. As a single woman in a very tough business, she was obviously as hard as nails. I think over a couple of drinks in a bar, she'd be great fun.

FRED: We heard the song was banned in North Korea, because cats have a holy status there, as do cows in India.

RICH: They also asked if they could change the word 'sexy' to 'fancy' or 'happy', which we refused to do, obviously.

FRED: Back in the UK, the plan was to sign a deal with a major label, but we decided to stay with Tug Records. We signed a three-album deal in December 1991. It all went sour with them not long afterwards, and I think part of the reason we fell out with them was because they were forced into signing a deal that wasn't great for them. We had had hits with our first two singles, so we had them up against the wall. They had to offer us preferential terms because the major labels were steaming in with their cheque books.

RICH: Even so, why on earth did we do that?

FRED: Better the devil you know, I guess. To be fair, I still think it was the right decision, because we'd built up some momentum with the current team – and staying as independent as possible appealed to us.

RICH: Well, hindsight is always 20/20.

FRED: True. By mid-1992 we had become household names, just like that, and we were everywhere, especially in tabloid newspapers. They went fucking bonkers, mostly because of the way we looked and Richard's sexuality. We found that funny, and bizarre, and we embraced it. We knew that we'd been given a golden opportunity, after years of working in the shadows, so we played the game. We behaved ourselves. We turned up to events and we did what we were asked to do.

RICH: Pretty soon it was just about keeping the record company happy, even though keeping the company happy is not an artist's job.

FRED: A lot of managers and record companies aren't very empathetic. The very thing that's making them money is the very thing they want to run into the ground.

RICH: We know that sometimes we were difficult to work with, mainly due to lack of sleep and overwork. It's a marathon, not a sprint – but nobody seemed to get that. I remember biting Tamzin's head off once, when we landed in Birmingham after some promotion in Europe. I was utterly exhausted, so when she came up and said, 'Hi, Rich, how are you?' I said, 'I'm fucking knackered, you daft cow.'

FRED: Ouch, poor old Tamzin. She got it in the neck when we were tired, didn't she?

RICH: I know that sounds unreasonable, but she wasn't going on the road with us, and therefore just didn't get it. That's the problem with nearly every manager we've ever had, and every record company we've ever dealt with. They don't have a fucking clue what it's like to be on the road. I don't just mean touring, I mean the promotional work as well. They've got a complete and utter disconnect from that, and they don't understand that side of the industry they're in. But I'm sorry I spoke to Tamzin like that. I hope she reads this and understands that I was just exhausted.

FRED: Despite all the record sales, and TV, and all the stuff we did in 1991 and '92, the industry still didn't get us, which is why we've never really been embraced by them. We don't fit in. It may be that they don't know what the fuck to do with us. Or maybe, because we recorded a song as big as 'Sexy' that all the record labels turned down, it made them look pretty stupid. Perhaps they've never forgiven us for that? I've always believed that the music industry and the music business are two separate entities with different goals. A lot of managers and record labels assume all artists want the same things – fame and money. That simply isn't true.

RICH: A guy came up to us a few years ago at the Cannes Film Festival and said, 'I was on the Mercury Awards committee for years, and everyone now talks about how you should have got that award, because your album *Up* was the breakout LP of that year.' It's disappointing – but to be honest it's neither here nor there. We make a good living getting to do what we love.

FRED: The Radio 1 DJ Peter Powell came up to me at some club when we were playing 'Sexy', way before it was huge. He said, 'Did you write this song?' I said yes, and he said, 'You'll never be poor.'

RICH: If I hadn't come up with the line 'I'm too sexy for my shirt', who knows where we'd be now?

FRED: Probably still working in a gym, maybe reminiscing about all the people we worked with in these last two chapters, but without the happy ending.

RICH: I do like a happy ending.

FRED: Steady on.

RICH: Sometimes it feels like 'Sexy' is never going to go away. Did you know Tom Hanks did a parody video of it for *Saturday Night Live* in 2014? It was called 'Please Don't Cut My Testicles'.

FRED: Brilliant. William Shatner sang it too, believe it or not. It was a karaoke scene in a show called *Shit My Dad Says*. Captain Kirk sang our song!

RICH: Cameron Diaz and Christina Applegate did it as well, in the film *The Sweetest Thing*, although they changed the lyrics so they were singing about penis size. Fair enough, I reckon.

FRED: And it was in *The West Wing*.

RICH: Really?

FRED: Yes, a character called CJ started singing it in an episode that went out in about 2001.

RICH: Bloody hell, I never saw that coming.

Deeply Dippy
Fairbrass/Fairbrass/Manzoli (1992)
Reprinted with permission from Spirit Music Group

Deeply dippy about the curves you got
Deeply hot, hot for the curves you've got
Deeply dippy about the fun we had
Deeply mad, mad for the fun we had

Oh, my love, I can't make head nor tail of passion
Oh, my love, let's set sail for seas of passion now

Deeply dippy about the way you walk
Contact sport, let the neighbours talk
Deeply dippy, I'm your Superman
I'll explain you're my Lois Lane

Oh, my love, I can't make head nor tail of passion
Oh, my love, let's set sail for seas of passion now

Deeply dippy about your Spanish eyes,
Sierra smile, legs that go on for miles and miles...
Oh, see those legs, man, miles and miles
Oh, my love, I can't make head nor tail of passion
Oh, my love, let's set sail for seas of passion now

FRED: 'Deeply Dippy' is about infatuation. I remember playing it to a friend on an acoustic guitar, and he said, 'That's a hit record.' He was right – it went to number one. Still, we were surprised by how big a hit this song was, considering the first two singles had been dance tracks.

RICH: I really like these lyrics. A TV presenter told us that he thought this song was a guaranteed hit. I wasn't sure, though. I remember sitting in a radio station, waiting to be interviewed, and the song 'Insanity' by Oceanic was playing, which was a banging track. It sounded amazing. 'Deeply Dippy' starts with just a solo acoustic guitar, and I thought, 'We're fucked.'

Chapter 4

The View from the Top

So what's it like to be a pop star? Funny you should ask.

RICH: Let's talk about 1991 to 1994.

FRED: Okay.

RICH: After that we can talk about how it all went wrong again.

FRED: That's no fun. Can we at least get Steve Tandy to talk for a bit?

RICH: We definitely can. Steve is a radio plugger. For those who don't know, a radio plugger takes tracks to radio stations, trying to convince the DJs to play them – or, even better, add the song to their play list. Over to you, Steve...

STEVE TANDY: Hello! I was working regional radio at my first plugging company, Station to Station. Regional radio was really small in those days. In fact, no one was really taking it seriously because it was so tiny. My first contact with Right Said Fred came when my boss, Martin Levitt, played a cassette of 'I'm Too Sexy' in the office, and I went along to see you perform at the Black Cap in Camden. It was a weekday night, and there was about twenty people in the audience. I remember thinking, this song is either going to die on its arse, or it's going to be huge – one or the other.

FRED: The former... yay!

RICH: Yay indeed.

STEVE: So I took you two and Rob Manzoli to see Steve Allen at the radio station LBC, because he was a Right Said Fred fan very early on. After that I gave you, Rich, a lift home in my Ford Orion. I remember you sitting there and saying, 'I like this car. If we make some money, I might get one of these.' Fast-forward two years and you were huge. I met you again when we were doing promo, and I was still driving my Ford Orion – and you both had TVRs!

RICH: I was probably just being polite. We're nice like that.

FRED: What were we like as people back then, Steve?

STEVE: I thought you were very grounded, and Rob too. You'd been at it a while, and like a lot of artists, you probably thought it was never going to happen, so when it hit, I think you were genuinely surprised. You were always very easy to work with.

FRED: Well, that's nice to hear. We obviously hadn't turned into complete cunts yet.

RICH: That came later. Anyway, I've always been a low-maintenance kind of guy. I'm pretty relaxed, generally. You're much more hands-on with the business of the band than I am, Fred. You play more of a management role because you've always been motivated in that way.

STEVE: We had some good times back then. I remember we did a radio tour in a Winnebago, which is a very large vehicle that is designed to go in straight lines down American motorways, but it wouldn't fit in your road in Fulham because of all the cars parked there.

FRED: That kind of expensive fuck-up happened all the time back then. Why on earth would the record label hire a Winnebago to drive around the narrow streets of London?

RICH: Still, we had a lot of laughs. The first few months of success were a breeze, after all those years of obscurity. Enjoying performances only really hit me when 'Sexy' happened – the idea of being a frontman grew on me.

FRED: Yes. We should be clear that it was a lot of fun at first. We recorded our first album, *Up*, on the back of 'I'm Too Sexy' and 'Don't Talk Just Kiss', so there was a limited recording budget. The album needed to get finished, so we were doing very long studio sessions – and when the musicians had to stay late we said, 'We don't have any more money, but we've got some coke.'

RICH: We were still a long way from being well off, but we were definitely much better off than on our first tour in 1978 where we had no money for food. Back in those days we would stop at motorway cafes, sit next to a table that had lots of food and wait for the customers to leave, then eat their leftovers. The problem with this plan was that sometimes we'd have to start with desserts and end on what was left of a prawn cocktail.

FRED: For the whole period between 'Sexy' coming out in July '91 and the spring of '94, when the promo for the second album finished, we were constantly working. Playing shows, doings loads of TV and radio, recording, press and personal appearances. There were hardly any breaks during that time. On one occasion we were grumbling about being tired and someone rightly said to us, 'Well, you wanted it, now you've got it.' They were 100 per cent right.

RICH: We should have remembered the adage, 'Don't work hard, work smart'.

Survival Tip No. 9: **Sometimes the Press Can't Be Trusted**

RICH: We did an interview with the *NME* once. The journalist turned up, and his tape recorder wasn't working because the batteries were flat, so we asked our PA to pop out and grab some new batteries. When we read the article, he just ripped the shit out of us. Thanks, *NME* guy.

FRED: Some of the press were all right, though. I remember we were doing back-to-back interviews all day at a big promo event. Most of the journalists were asking us 'Are you really too sexy for your shirt?' or 'Can I feel your biceps?' and all this crap, and we were sick to death of it, but then this girl came in and started talking about music. She asked about guitar sounds, amps and our writing process, and we ended up having a good conversation about music. She was an absolute breath of fresh air. Most music journalists firmly believe that if you write a song like 'I'm Too Sexy' then you must be a bit dim. They're incapable of broadening their preconceptions.

RICH: All through the eighties we had been involved with one charity or another, so staying involved after the band broke was only natural. Do you remember *Tommy's Tape?*

FRED: Yes, that was a project in 1992 with Anneka Rice – she wanted different artists to make an entire album in three days. We recorded our song, 'When I See an Elephant Fly', with George Martin, who was wonderful. We were discussing the track and he said, 'We need a different drum sound.' He took the kick drum away and put a drum case there instead. He said we needed more of a skiffle sound. I admired the hell out of him.

FRED: The recording of *Up* was quite a fragmented process, as we were having to promote 'I'm Too Sexy' and then 'Don't Talk Just Kiss'. Becoming a household name was already starting to do our heads in by this point. We seemed to be popping up on every TV show imaginable. Through 1991 to 1993 we were being booked on TV shows that we should never really have done – it was a complete waste of time and money. Our tracks had already done great business, so we didn't need to be there. We should have been writing more songs and prepping for the next album. There was a complete absence of planning and vision from management and the record label.

RICH: The great misunderstanding is that being on TV is the most important thing.

FRED: It's only important if being famous is important to you. Weirdly, Tug Records seemed more motivated about fame than most artists I know.

RICH: The fame part of it was not that important to us. When it died down a few years later, we were quite happy with that. I remember chatting briefly with the singer Gabrielle, and reading between the lines of what she said, it seemed to me that fame was not that important to her either.

FRED: There was a lot of pointless promotion we should never have gone along with, not just in the UK but in lots of countries. We should have just done prime-time TV, then been out on the road doing the festival circuit and back in pre-production. Maybe the record company thought it was branding – I don't really know. I know their job is artist exposure, which we had no issue with, but it was definitely quantity over quality.

RICH: We bumped into Michael Stipe from R.E.M. just before our first US tour. He asked if we'd toured the US yet, and we told him no. He looked at us with fear in his eyes and said, 'It's fucking terrifying, man.' That's always stayed with me.

FRED: I remember that very well – he had tiny, round red sunglasses on.

RICH: Pretty soon other stars started asking to meet us.

FRED: I remember this guy came up to me at Green Onions, a club in Kensington, and said that he worked with Prince. He said, 'Prince is downstairs and he'd like to meet you.' So I went down there and there he was, sitting there with these two big blokes. He said, 'It's lovely to meet you,' but when I went to shake his hand, one of the bouncers pushed me back. They didn't want me to touch him. Still, Prince was very complimentary about our music, which was great to hear.

RICH: Speaking of Prince, we were special guests on the opening night of his club Glam in Osaka in Japan.

FRED: Working in Japan could be bizarre. On one TV show there was a bath of extremely hot water. The idea was that they'd lower a fan into the bath, and depending on how long she could tolerate the heat, that determined how long they'd play the 'I'm Too Sexy' video for. This poor girl started to scream after about thirty seconds and seemed very distressed. They pulled her out and she was lobster-red, so they wrapped her in foil, put her on a gurney and took her away. The audience loved it – they were clapping and jumping up and down.

RICH: Another time, on a TV show in Japan, they wanted us to perform and jump through flames. The discussion between our tour manager and the TV production got very heated, pun intended. Wally, our tour manager, was concerned about the potential safety issues. Eventually he went on set to take a look – and all became apparent. There were lots of picture frames suspended from the ceiling. They meant 'frames', not 'flames'. Lost in translation.

FRED: We never dreamt we'd become celebrities on this scale. We just thought 'Sexy' was a cool song – we didn't really overthink it. Our PR at the time told us that apart from Lady Diana, we were the most photographed Brits in the world. I don't know how true that is, but even if it's not true, it certainly felt like it.

RICH: Back in the US, after a show in Miami, we were invited to Mickey Rourke's bar, the Spot. Johnny Depp was also there, and we sat around and had drinks. I didn't think it was that great as experiences go. It felt like we were in a fishbowl, with everyone looking at you while you sit there and drink. The whole thing was a bit silly. Johnny Depp didn't like it either, so he left, but both he and Mickey Rourke were very friendly.

FRED: As time passed, we encountered a lot of famous people. One of them was Michael Hutchence of INXS, who we knew from doing promo. We first met him at the World Music Awards in Cannes, and then we bumped into him many times at different hotels. I hung out with him a little bit at Brown's club and we had a few drinks. One time I was particularly high and particularly bad-tempered, and I hit someone in Brown's – and that person landed on Michael. His reaction, along with that of the bouncer, was, 'I think you'd better leave.' But he was very friendly, as was Paula Yates. It's interesting – I was her local minicab driver back in the early eighties. She was incredibly nice, and then we met her again when we were doing that interview on the big bed for *The Big Breakfast.*

RICH: We met Robbie Williams many times over the years. We first met him when he was touring in Take That. Of that lot, Mark Owen was all right. Gary Barlow and the others were very standoffish. Robbie was always witty and approachable.

FRED: Then there's Ben Becker, a well-known actor in Germany. He joined us on stage on quite a few occasions and would climb up the lighting rig and swing from it. He would run around the stage like a madman. He was a bit of a fan, so we hung out with him quite a few times and partied with him.

RICH: Jason Donovan's a really nice guy too. We were doing a gig once, and he said, 'You want me to take some pictures?' I said yes, and while I was standing on stage, singing with my legs apart, he came flying under my legs, lying on a skateboard and taking photos.

FRED: With a lot of famous people, you just smile and have some laughs and a drink and it's no more than that. Kylie Minogue, Bernard Cribbins, John Travolta, Brian Glover, Ray Liotta... a lot of people. At first we did a lot of red carpet and VIP events, but after a while we got tired of it and stopped.

RICH: We first met Eddie Kidd in a nightclub around 1991. When we were kids, he was like a god to us, as he was to every kid in the seventies. He's been a great friend over the years, and it's a huge honour for us that he's written the foreword to this book.

FRED: Mind you, there's all sorts of stuff we can't tell you – like the supposedly straight male pop star who we saw sucking off a well-known footballer in the lift of a luxury hotel in Birmingham. The lift doors opened, while a party was going on, and there the two of them were. A few other people saw this happen, not just us, but if we revealed who either of them were, we'd get killed.

RICH: All that said, we never played the fame game outside work. I think if we'd been in love with that side of the business, we would have stayed in LA, got an agent, rented an apartment and worked the room.

Survival Tip No. 10: **Carpe diem!**

RICH: Joel Silver, the film director, came to see us backstage after a show. He was interested in us being in the next *Die Hard* movie, but we were hammered and lost his number. Doh!

FRED: We did do Howard Stern's radio show while we were in the USA – twice.

RICH: He asked me, 'Was it when you sat on a whoopee cushion that you discovered you were gay?', which didn't make any sense to us then and doesn't make any sense now.

FRED: Stern did this amazing thing when we were on his show, though. Our second single in America was 'Deeply Dippy', but Charisma Records had forgotten to put our name on the CD artwork. He had the CD in his hand and he said, 'You've just saved this record company's ass by being number one everywhere, and this is the best they can do? Who are you working with at Charisma?' He phoned up the record company, got through to the label manager and made her apologise, live on air. She actually did it, and then the label fired her.

RICH: That was brutal.

FRED: Being famous in America was very different to being famous in the UK or Europe. The US entertainment business is on a huge scale, and fame is taken very seriously. We met the songwriter Cathy Dennis just before our US tour. She said, 'If you're not famous in the US, then you're not really famous at all.' At the time, we thought that sounded like bollocks – but having spent a lot of time in the US, we now know that she was 100 per cent right.

RICH: I must admit that global fame felt good. Finally, the faith we'd had in ourselves was being vindicated. We'd been right all along. Every fucking label that had turned us down was now being proved wrong, which felt very good indeed.

FRED: Not that we blame them for turning 'Sexy' down – it was pretty left-field.

RICH: 'I'm Too Sexy' was an outside-the-box song, not just for the audience but also for us. We'd been on the live circuit for over a decade, playing styles of music that were very different to 'Sexy'. Suddenly we had a hit record that sounded nothing like anything we'd done before.

RICH: Right Said Fred was never well suited to being in the showbiz machine. We could have made a much better fist of it, but we prefer to maintain a happy work–life balance.

FRED: When I'm on my deathbed, I won't be thinking, 'If only we'd done more TV!'

RICH: You and I are neighbourhood guys – we like familiar faces and places.

FRED: Maybe if we'd been based in New York instead of LA we would have spent more time in the US. I also liked Austin – it had a good vibe.

RICH: Yes, but I just wanted to go home. I remember talking to our tour manager, Wally Versen, and asking him, 'How long am I going to be here? I just want to go home.' It was partly because I was missing Stuart, partly because of his ill-health, and partly because I wanted to see familiar surroundings – I guess it was a bit of everything, really. I remember JJ Cale saying something along the lines of, 'What's the point of promoting a song that's already been a hit? I might as well be at home.'

FRED: I think we would have felt differently if we were touring with a band and crew, as opposed to being cast as celebrities. We complained about this to one of the US tour managers. Even though 'I'm Too Sexy' was number one on the US college charts, his response was, 'You can't go out with a live band – there isn't the demand.' Yeah, right. That was our Spinal Tap moment.

RICH: If you're in a band, and you're connecting with an audience every night or every other night, that grounds you. It tells you where you are, and it tells you who you like, and who likes you, so it gives you a compass of some kind. But when you're just doing promo, waving at a camera, or in radio stations, you don't really know who your audience is, and you don't really know who or what you are.

Survival Tip No. 11: **The Artist Eventually Pays for Everything**

RICH: Learning to deal with financial matters was an eye-opener. I remember I met this cute guy in LA. The record company said I could keep the limo for the night, so he and I had a great night out and we ended up at a diner for breakfast.

About a year later, I got a bill for the limo rental. I realised then that there's no such thing as a free lunch – or a free limo.

FRED: In this business, if somebody offers you money, it's just a loan. You're going to have to pay it back one way or another.

RICH: We learned that lesson in the end.

FRED: On the road, we tried to keep sane by playing games. You and Rob had one game called 'What thing in this hotel room can we fit up your arse?' I think you or Rob initially experimented with a Trimphone... I also remember that you got a Toblerone out of the mini-fridge and gently inserted it into your bottom.

RICH: What can I say? I was bored. Afterwards, I pulled it out, partially melted, wrapped it up in the foil, slid it back into the packet and then put it back in the fridge. I've often wondered who stayed there next, and whether they got the midnight munchies.

FRED: I think alcohol may have played a part in these activities. Do you remember the prawns incident?

RICH: Oh, that was great. At one hotel, somewhere in Europe, we knew we'd be coming in late that day and leaving the next day before breakfast started, so we asked them to arrange a late dinner for us, which they promised to do. It was a five-star hotel, so we assumed they'd do a good job. As agreed, they'd left some prawns for us – but they stank to high heaven, and didn't look too clever either. They'd clearly been sitting there for hours, and no way could we eat them. Before we left the following morning, we put the prawns in the air-conditioning.

FRED: You do get a bit unruly on the road. That's partly because you're allowed to be. I think some people get disappointed when bands don't misbehave.

RICH: It's a surreal existence out there. The sense of not belonging was a problem for us.

FRED: We did a show in Boston with James Brown, but Rob forgot his guitar.

RICH: He literally had one thing to remember – his fucking guitar! – and he forgot it.

FRED: He found a mannequin backstage, took its leg off, and mimed with that.

RICH: James Brown's limo pulled up at the side of the stage, and he performed for about twenty minutes and then left. The driver kept the engine running the whole time. James was dressed in a tight, Kermit-green suit. A lot of the time he wasn't singing, he was just enjoying the band, who – not unsurprisingly – were great. He had a real swagger about him: he was full of confidence.

FRED: We loved that.

RICH: Back in the UK I was awarded something called Rear of the Year. They sent me a commemorative silver engraved plate, and I sent it back – which now seems a bit churlish. I think the celebrity tag was just driving us nuts by this point.

FRED: We had become celebs and couldn't stand the culture of it.

RICH: We just didn't like the fakeness of it all.

FRED: We found ourselves saying fuck this, fuck that and fuck you too often. That's not a good place to be.

RICH: Sometimes we still say that now.

FRED: As time passed it became apparent that our most faithful fans weren't all in the UK. Germany, Belgium, Austria, Holland, South Africa, South America, as well as Canada and parts of the USA, proved to be very faithful.

RICH: Those are still good markets for us.

FRED: One of the first European TV shows we did was in a little studio in Italy. There were two cameras – but only one cameraman. One camera was locked off and we were told not to move around. The solitary cameraman was running between the two cameras, and we were a tad naive back then, so we went along with the chaos. At one point we asked for the backing track to be much louder, at which point one of the wall-mounted speakers came loose and crashed to the floor, ripping the speaker cables out. We assumed we'd be redoing the shoot, but no, the cameraman shouted 'Non fermarti, non fermarti! Continua, continua!' Rob is half Italian and got the gist of what he meant – so we 'continua, continua'.

Survival Tip No. 12: Never Defer

RICH: At some point back then, we did a show in Leicester Square, and the sound guy said, 'Do you want any particular music to be played as you come on?' We said, 'No, mate, play whatever you like,' and as we stood side of stage we heard the theme to *Match of the Day* blasting across the club. Nowadays we're much more demanding. We want everything agreed beforehand in the contract. The devil is in the detail.

FRED: 'Deeply Dippy' was released in March 1992. It was a departure for us and opened up a brand-new audience. You and I wrote the chorus, and Rob came up with that cool little guitar part. Molly Duncan from the Average White Band arranged the brass parts. He did a truly outstanding job; I love that brass arrangement to this day. In fact, the house band for *The Arsenio Hall Show* asked us to send compliments to Molly for his arrangement.

RICH: Chuck Sabo on drums and Phil Spalding on bass made an excellent rhythm section. Molly's brass arrangement was the cherry on top.

FRED: 'Deeply Dippy' helped take our debut album, *Up*, straight to number one in March 1992. We were an inescapable presence in the UK at this point. I guess you could say we'd become family favourites.

RICH: Although our relationship with Tug Records was often fractious, the success of 'Deeply Dippy' and the first album gave us all cause to celebrate. Mind you, we weren't everyone's favourite. We were in the Reflex club in Putney shortly after the band broke, and two guys made a comment about us being 'faggots' as we walked by. I walked back, put one of them up against the wall with my forearm and asked him to repeat it. He didn't.

FRED: We tend to run out of patience very quickly in those situations.

RICH: We had a few altercations back then. Here's a notable one.

FRED: We were in Ibiza in 1993, staying at Pikes Hotel before doing an event. Pikes was an infamous luxury hotel where Freddie Mercury had had parties and where they shot Wham!'s 'Club Tropicana' video. I was walking back to my room one afternoon; it was very quiet as most people were having their siesta. It was then I saw a guy kick one of the hotel cats into the pool. I decided to take revenge.

Later that night, dinner was by the pool. We had made friends with Dave of The Dave Clark Five, who was a bit handy because he was martial arts-trained. I told Dave about the cat, and he said, 'If you see the cunt, let's sort him out.' The guy turned up for dinner dressed head to toe in leather – he even had the tassels up the outside of his trousers, with cowboy boots and all the trimmings. I said to Dave, 'There he is.' We walked up to him and Dave was all smiles – and I knocked the guy into the pool. He was fucking furious, and over the next few days it all kicked off. People were complaining about us, although they eventually calmed down when they were told about the cat.

When we got home, a letter arrived from Anthony Pike, the hotel owner, calling us 'bald-headed hooligans' and saying that he'd spoken to the police and that we were now banned from Ibiza for the next three years. We did write back to Tony and explain the circumstances, but he didn't respond. He died not long ago.

RICH: What a heartwarming story! Now back to 1992.

FRED: We were approached by *Baywatch* around this time. They wanted us to play the house band on the beach. We had a meeting with Pamela Anderson, who was one of the show's producers at the time, and she loved the idea.

RICH: Why did she want to meet us in person?

FRED: I think she felt it was important that she met us and liked us, because it was going to be a regular thing for us. Then we were told they'd lost their syndication, at which point we were advised to stay away because it looked like it was going to be cancelled. David Hasselhoff then apparently bought the rights, and the show – as we all know – then became very successful. He'd had the initiative to say, 'Actually, we can make this work.' He had brilliant vision.

RICH: I rarely enjoy doing TV because it tends to be antiseptic, with the exception of live TV shows. When there's an audience right behind the cameras it suddenly turns into a 'show'. Still, we appeared on *Wogan* shortly before 'Deeply Dippy' was released – the audience and Terry Wogan himself were great.

FRED: We returned to the US and Canada to start an in-store tour. For those who don't know what an in-store is, it's when an artist does an appearance and sometimes a performance inside a record shop, before doing an autograph session. These can generate huge interest in the artist and their songs. We like them because we get to meet the audience one to one. When we did an in-store at Tower Records in New York, we apparently drew more people than Prince or Madonna. It was a crazy experience – they had to redirect traffic around Broadway for a few hours.

RICH: A lot of American radio stations wouldn't stop playing 'I'm Too Sexy', which we were told was selling 100,000 copies a day. If that was the case, there was little motivation for the label to release the *Up* album or a follow-up single, which was really frustrating for us. We had started to realise that, bit by bit, this celebrity thing had taken over, no matter where we played or what we released.

FRED: By now our celebrity status had us by the balls, not just in the UK, but all over the world. We did *Live with Regis and Kathie Lee* in New York, which is one of the biggest American morning-TV shows. They had no idea what we did. I said, 'Why are we here?' They said, 'Because you're famous,' and we replied, 'What the fuck do you mean?' They said, 'Our booker told us that you're really hot property.' They didn't know we were musicians. We thought this was fucking stupid. We could have been on there for any reason – being famous was the only criterion.

RICH: Fortunately we had developed thick skins, thanks to all the work we'd done in the early days. I remember when we were first doing club appearances after 'I'm Too Sexy' broke, we performed a PA at a club where there was no stage, so we stood in the middle of the room with the audience all around us. The CD started jumping as I sang, so we had to stop. The audience got very hostile, but if you buckle in that situation, you're fucked. I said, 'You can see there's no band, so it's fucking obvious the music is running off a CD. Grow up and we'll start again!' The audience really liked that attitude. Previous experiences like that enabled us to deal with these situations.

FRED: There's an old clip online of JJ Cale playing with Eric Clapton, and JJ really fucks up a couple of notes, but he's unfazed. He just carries on playing – and that's what you've got to learn to do.

RICH: On which note, quite a few rockers used to like our music for some reason.

FRED: Yes, that's true. One of our tour managers in the US, who'd worked with Guns N' Roses said they'd been in a car when 'I'm Too Sexy' was on the radio. They pulled over at a record store and bought the single.

RICH: 'Sexy' really did seem to cross a lot of boundaries.

FRED: A few years later, the DJ Jason Nevins asked if we wanted to do a remix of 'I'm Too Sexy' with him. He said that Slash was interested in playing on it but had to pull out due to other commitments, so he spoke to Dave Navarro, who said he'd do it. We got Dave's mobile number and called him, but we got his answerphone. The message was: 'It's Dave Navarro, I'm out in my car-o.' Seriously... Anyway, he went on the road with the Red Hot Chili Peppers and that was that.

RICH: I think we started to unravel very quickly. We were in Germany in about '94 at a press conference, and for some reason we would only talk in falsetto. We were absolutely exhausted and couldn't take any of it seriously any more. Why we chose falsetto I have no idea. Tug Records were so fucking angry with us.

FRED: Absolutely, but we weren't in our right minds. We were slowly going crazy.

RICH: When we first did kids' TV, the record company told me that I had to shave my chest because a hairy chest would frighten the children. I agreed to do it, because I assumed they knew what they were doing. They also told me that I could never reveal that Stuart was my partner – they were obsessed with that. I deferred to them on that, because I thought they knew the market better than me. What I should have done was told them to fuck off.

FRED: Also, very few gay artists were out of the closet at the time. Everyone was so on edge about you being gay – they were such idiots.

RICH: The tipping point for us was when we appeared on the Royal Variety Performance show in 1993 with the Muppets. If I had been watching us at that point, I'd be thinking, 'What the fuck are they on?' That said, it was great to meet the Queen afterwards. She was very nice. I made her laugh. She asked, 'Are you brothers?' and I said, 'That's what Mum says,' and she giggled. Meeting her meant more to Mum than it meant to us, and needless to say, it was the official stamp of approval as far as our relatives were concerned.

FRED: I think we were the real muppets, agreeing to do that show in that way.

RICH: I suppose the psychological wheels came off for us at this point. Our relationship with Rob and the record label were also deteriorating quickly.

FRED: Rob and I never really got along that well – Rich was the cream in the Oreo, so to speak.

RICH: When you have hits, it's a team effort, and there are lots of people involved. The problem is, you don't know who's responsible for the track's success – is it you, is it your manager, is it the record label, or a combination of all three? You're left feeling insecure about not only your role in that success but also other people's. For us, it was only when the wheels started falling off that we could see who was an asset and who was a liability.

FRED: For the first two years, we did pretty much what we were told: when the label said, 'Jump,' we said, 'How high?'

There was a fourth single from *Up*, which was a double A-side of 'Those Simple Things' and a cover of The Lovin' Spoonful's 'Daydream'. By the time we started writing the second album, it felt too much like a job. The fun was evaporating very fast.

RICH: People didn't know what to make of us. We and 'I'm Too Sexy' came out of nowhere. Usually with a new band there's gossip within the business, but that hadn't happened with us. There was no advance warning.

FRED: I think a lot of it had to do with the way we looked. We weren't really made aware of that until we started doing shows with other artists. We were used to going to gyms and being surrounded by big blokes, but when we did *Top of the Pops*, it hit us like a train how different we looked. We didn't fit in, but it didn't bother us – in fact we liked it. The music business didn't know how to react to us, and we didn't know how to react to them, especially knowing that just a few months earlier they all thought we were dead in the water.

RICH: Basically, our success ran away completely. Neither the label nor our manager had the skills or experience to deal with it. They were out of their depth, as were we: more experienced people might have coped with it better. Look at some of the terrible deals we signed.

FRED: The merch deal was an absolute disaster, signing off for twenty-five grand worldwide. Our advance should have been huge and we should have been getting a cut.

RICH: We didn't really have a clue, did we?

FRED: In all fairness, there's nothing to say that another label would have handled the business any worse or better than Tug Records did. There will be successes and failures wherever you go. Still, we could tell things weren't particularly well organised. Every day appeared to be a surprise for Tug: they seemed to have no strategy. There was no: 'Okay, everyone take a breath, we're going to put this whole thing together and get it right.' It was just panic stations every day.

RICH: Fortunately, we didn't usually have to deal with the label ourselves.

FRED: We rarely saw them, and we didn't really engage with them on any level. Tamzin was our point of contact when it came to what we did every day. For her age, she did extraordinarily well. She was a good pair of hands in terms of making things run properly, but she wasn't a decision-maker.

RICH: One thing we did like was the licensing aspect – that appealed to us very early on. The idea of getting our music out to different countries with a simple agreement was very attractive.

FRED: That said, they really fucked up France and Japan, because they put us on Virgin Records, who were sacking a shedload of people at the time. None of the people there knew if they'd have a job in six months' time, which was horrible. It was really hard in Germany too: they put us on a label who had never released a record. They were just a mail-order company, although Germany became a great market for us once we signed with Intercord. On the other hand, the label in Belgium and Holland were really good. All the labels in northern Europe did a very good job, but Spain and Italy, not so much. Australia, South America and Canada also worked out well. So overall, the licensing was pretty good.

RICH: Thank God for that.

FRED: By the end of 1992 they wanted to hear tracks for the second album, which was a joke because we'd had no time to write. We were knackered, and also I couldn't even be in the same room as the label without wanting to kill someone.

RICH: We should really have made the second album at the same time as the first one. I'm serious, I read that The Stranglers did that. It's a very smart thing to do.

FRED: I agree. Maybe we should have just walked away and had another meeting with Peter Gross.

RICH: I wish we had. Do you remember Faith No More wanted us to tour with them around this time?

FRED: I have a quote from their singer Mike Patton right here. He told *Sky* magazine in 1992, 'We wanted them to tour America with us. Maybe it's the baldness – they're so slick. They're crass, commercial and goofy at the same time. They're amazing. Also the fact that they worked in a gym is great. I love that.'

RICH: Why didn't we do it?

FRED: I can't remember.

RICH: So what did we do instead? Go straight into the second album!

FRED: We must have been totally out of our minds.

RICH: We had precious little time to write new songs through this period, and it was really starting to piss us off. We just knew that the label were going to say, 'When can we hear the new album?' Artists forget that they're self-employed. We should have had the nuts to say, 'We're taking time out, so the album can wait.' Do you remember when someone at Tug Records said, 'Can't you write in between interviews, in the back of cabs or in hotel rooms?' They really didn't have a clue, so we're back to the huge chasm between the music business and the music industry.

FRED: The record label sent us Madonna's *Erotica* album and said, 'This is the album you're going to make.' What they should have done, of course, is send us our first album – because that had proved to be very successful.

RICH: By the time I woke up and realised that we'd been played, it wasn't too late, but it still pissed me off.

FRED: So we recorded our second album, *Sex and Travel.* That was an expensive and laborious process. Our relationships with virtually everyone around us were falling apart, and we were tired when we recorded it. As difficult as Tommy D was to work with, we shouldn't have split up a winning team – stupidly we did. *Up* had worked well with Phil Spalding on bass, Chuck Sabo on drums, Tommy on programming and production, and Graham Bonnet as the studio engineer. Graham's contribution is highly underrated – without his production experience the album wouldn't have sounded nearly as good as it does. We and Tommy were lucky to have Graham on board.

RICH: Of course, the fact that we didn't have any songs didn't matter to the label. As we mentioned, they said, 'Why don't you do the songwriting while you're in a taxi between interviews?' Yes, they actually said that.

FRED: In one meeting they said, 'You guys could record the telephone directory and have a hit album.' As it turned out, we probably should have done that.

RICH: They meant it as a compliment, but if you believe even a tiny bit of that compliment, it's a problem. What the label should have said is, 'Just make the first album again. Use the same producer and the same people.' If it ain't broke, don't fix it.

FRED: We booked out some time at a hotel to get the songs written. I didn't want us writing at my place again because Rob was a heavy smoker, and we couldn't write at your place because of Stuart. We looked at studios, but they're expensive, so we ended up hiring a room in a hotel.

RICH: It worked out much cheaper than a studio.

FRED: Before *Sex and Travel* was recorded, we wrote a song for

Comic Relief. That was in March 1993. I enjoyed recording the song, which was 'Stick It Out'. The video was fun – we had Peter Cook, Lennox Lewis, Hugh Laurie and Jools Holland taking part.

RICH: During the writing of 'Stick It Out', we were in a hotel room with Richard Curtis. The phone rang and that was when the funding came through for *Four Weddings and a Funeral.*

FRED: He was very happy, although he didn't tell us how much it was.

RICH: I wish we hadn't done Comic Relief at that point. We'd been on the road constantly for over two years and we should have taken a break.

FRED: Needless to say, we didn't.

RICH: No wonder *Sex and Travel* wasn't fun.

FRED: Well, we didn't enjoy making it. There were too many drugs going on, and there was too much animosity between everyone. The producer, Robin Goodfellow, had had some success with East 17. He's a very nice guy, but at that time he seemed to have had his own personal issues, and as a band we were done.

RICH: Do we sound like we're complaining a lot about being tired?

FRED: Probably, but it was explained to us once that between 1991 and '94 we did promo in thirty countries and took less than a month off in that time. I'd call those reasonable grounds for being knackered.

RICH: Well, when you put it like that...

FRED: Some of the songwriting on *Sex and Travel* is very good. 'Hands Up for Lovers', 'We Live a Life', 'Rocket Town' and 'She's My Mrs' are all decent songs.

RICH: I notice you're not mentioning any of the singles. 'Bumped' is a good song.

FRED: I liked 'Bumped' a lot. Remember 'Wonderman'? Whose idea was it to get involved with Sonic the fucking Hedgehog?

RICH: Not ours.

FRED: Sony asked us if they could rework that song for the new Sonic video game, and they offered us a healthy fee, so we said yes. You have to understand, we were going mad at this point.

RICH: Our judgement had completely lapsed. When everything is chaos, nothing makes sense, so you just say yes to everything to avoid facing that fact.

FRED: We were just sick of everything, so as one shit idea after another came our way, if it made money we just shrugged our shoulders and said yes. We didn't know what else to do.

RICH: After *Sex and Travel*, Tamzin quit. We don't blame her; the atmosphere was horrible.

FRED: The whole thing was starting to fall apart, and there was a part of me that was happy to see it fall apart. I didn't want to be involved in it. You know, thank you and good night.

RICH: Didn't we record a song called 'You're a Cunt' and send it to Tug Records?

FRED: Indeed we did. Funnily enough, radio wouldn't play it... shocker.

RICH: Everyone was expecting the second album to be huge, but it wasn't. Let's be honest, the sound of the whole album was wrong.

FRED: It was too serious and nowhere near playful enough. At this point our relationship with Tug Records was beyond repair. We thought we were going to like being successful, but it took me a while to get my head around it. I was disappointed in myself at times. I'd had visions of being a certain kind of pop star, but I didn't realise the hoops I was expected to jump through.

RICH: Too many hoops, man.

FRED: The nice house, the car and the money were all enjoyable, but the circus that came with it just isn't us. We just wanted to play our music on stage and be left the fuck alone, but that's difficult with an image like ours. Just to make things more surreal, in September 1993 I married Louise Payne, who at the time was a Page Three model. Getting married was a dumb idea – my head and heart weren't in the right place.

RICH: Stuart and Louise didn't get on. I remember we were all in a hotel in Amsterdam, and you and Louise were waiting for us at the bar. When Stuart and I came down, you said, 'I've just asked Louise to marry me' – and you should have seen Stuart's face. As we went back upstairs, he said, 'What the fuck is Fred doing?'

FRED: Louise and I were all over the media – the wedding was even on the *Six O'Clock News*. The whole thing was a circus from beginning to end. Louise was a nice person – it's just that we shouldn't have got married.

RICH: So why did you?

FRED: I was in the mindset that everything I did was going to succeed, and if I said, 'I like you, let's get married,' then it would be absolutely fine. Of course, it wasn't fine. The relationship with Louise went off the rails very quickly, although we hung in there for a year or so. The divorce was relatively painless, although the press had some fun at my expense, of course. They said some pretty funny things, like, 'He's had to sell his Fulham mansion and now lives in a small cottage.' One of the papers even tried a honey trap, sending a scantily dressed girl round to my house thinking that I'd let her in and tell all.

RICH: The press loved us and hated us. It was bizarre. People in the industry were generally very stereotypical in their thinking back then. They thought the combination of 'I'm Too Sexy' and having muscles guaranteed a gay audience. I remember we went to some awards show and I was told that I shouldn't mention coming out. I'm not sure if it was simple homophobia, or because they wanted me to seem available to women, as a marketing ploy.

FRED: Who knows? The record label was very twitchy about the 'gay' thing.

RICH: When you start off, you assume everybody knows more than you do, but of course, the truth is that they don't. The great thing about art is that it's completely subjective. We used to know a guy who thought The Beatles were shit but was a huge Rolling Stones fan. It's horses for courses.

FRED: Some artists absolutely love the screaming girls and the mayhem, but we didn't. At this point I felt complete and utter contempt for the music business and all who sail in her. I was stunned by what wankers some musicians and record company people are. Naively I thought it would be one big happy gang, but it was hostile, bitchy, jealous and shallow. I was genuinely stunned. You can work with some musicians for many years, and the moment you stop paying them, you'll never hear from them again.

RICH: You know, JJ Cale said he wanted the money without the fame, and that's basically my position too. One of the lessons I learned really early on is that fame is transitory. When the band first broke, I bought a house and I was kitting out the bathroom. I went into this local bathroom showroom to buy the bath and a sink and all that kind of stuff. We'd just been on *Top of the Pops* and 'Sexy' was huge, so there was definitely a part of me that was feeling a little bit arrogant, I'm afraid. As I'm standing there, this bloke comes up to me and says, 'Can you sign this, please?' I said, 'Sure, shall I make it out to you?' He looked at me really strangely and said, 'No, I've just delivered some toilets. Would you mind signing the form?'

FRED: That'll learn yer. I had a girl tear up my autograph. She came up to me in Putney and said, 'Can I have your autograph?' and gave me a pad of paper. I signed it and she said, 'Oh, you're not Richard?' and tore it up and walked off.

RICH: I was doing an autograph for one bloke, and as I was doing it he said, 'My girlfriend loves you guys, but I think you're shit.'

FRED: Ha ha! Great. No wonder we walked away from it all in 1994.

RICH: Well, by then we could afford to. We didn't need a record company any more, let alone Tug Records.

FRED: Yes, it helped that by '94, we were pretty comfortable financially. 'Sexy', 'Don't Talk' and 'Deeply Dippy' had all been successful, and so had *Up*, so we could afford to walk away.

RICH: And we made sure we owned our songs.

FRED: We actually got wealthy rather fast, which was obviously enjoyable after years of doing shit jobs and always worrying about money. Royalty payments started coming in around September 1991. 'Sexy' was selling like crazy, and all of a sudden, we were cash-rich. The most money we'd ever seen before that was £3,500 for the publishing deal. I really enjoyed not being poor any more.

RICH: Thank God 'Sexy' did well, because we were fucking broke before that. Stuart and I were living in a rented flat in Putney, and it was so cold one winter, and we had so little money, that we put all the furniture on the fire to keep warm.

FRED: In early 1992, you, Rob and I each got initial payments of around £150,000, which enabled us to buy houses, but we still didn't really have the next step planned out. We never sat down with the label and said, 'Right, this is what we're going to do over the next six months or a year.' We should have done that, but the reason we didn't is that we weren't being very astute.

RICH: I bought a three-bedroom terraced house in London for £148,000. Christ knows what it would be worth nowadays.

FRED: I got very excited when I first had some money, and made some stupid purchases. I remember I bought a massive American-style fridge for seven grand without measuring the front door of my house first. It arrived, and of course it wouldn't go in. They told me that they'd have to take all the windows out to get it in, and I didn't want to do that, so the fridge sat outside my house for two weeks. In the end, I sold it to a local restaurant for £200. That was a quick learning curve.

RICH: It was nice having lots of money, but I never really had a hard-on about it. Being rich was never our goal. I will say that it's very nice not to worry about paying bills, and we never look at the cost of food in restaurants.

FRED: Apart from my fridge incident, we've always been careful with money. We've always ploughed most of what we earn back into the studio or recordings or touring.

RICH: And property.

FRED: Yes. I bought a seven-bedroom house in Brighton, right by the sea. It was a former hotel, and I had it all done up. It drove me nuts though, it was way too big. I could never find my phone, keys or inhaler.

RICH: I will admit that we've blown a lot of money on cars over the years.

FRED: No, you've blown a lot of money on cars over the years.

RICH: My favourite car was a Porsche 928 with a cream leather interior, which I sold for some stupid reason. Then I bought a two-door Daimler, a really old one. That was a lovely car. After that I had a Jaguar E-Type. Nowadays the main car that we use is an Audi. I also have a BMW 8 Series: its engine has six litres and it's smooth as fuck.

FRED: I had a TVR, then a BMW 3 Series that I liked. Because of my equipment I went for Shoguns for a while, with the short wheelbase. Then I had a BMW X5, a Mercedes-AMG and a Range Rover Sports – I went all 'Jeepy' for a while. At the moment I've got a Porsche Cayman.

RICH: We tend to spend money when we haven't got it. When money looks like it might be running out, I buy things, which I know sounds like completely the wrong way around. But I only worry about money when it's not there. Most of the time, I try to live my life without thinking about it.

FRED: That's because you leave that to me.

RICH: We had a fortune by the mid-2000s, but we decided that we weren't so in love with it that we had to hang on to it. We were quite happy to spend it on recording, and we also bought a disability-friendly apartment in London for Stuart.

FRED: That was a lovely little flat.

RICH: I bought my first house in Fulham and lived there for ten years with Stuart, but we had a falling out and he moved out. I sold the Fulham house and moved into a flat in Chelsea. I bought that flat for £850,000 and sold it for £1.6 million – it was sheer luck.

FRED: I got into designer clothes for a while, and we treated ourselves to Rolex watches and some nice holidays.

RICH: We were over-generous to some of the people we worked with. That was a mistake. One person that we gave ten grand to as a parting gift denied that we'd ever done it. And we even lent him money! It was a joke.

FRED: To me, if you've got anything that you don't use, or property that you don't live in, it's just another headache. If I had a boat somewhere, for example, I'd be worried about it. As for houses, you can only inhabit one room at a time. We weren't divas about money.

RICH: The only time I get even remotely diva-ish – and I know this sounds corny – is if we're not being treated properly. We went to LA to do a gig a couple of years ago, and the minute we got to the airport and I saw that the driver hadn't put the seats down for the luggage, I knew it was going to be shit, because they weren't thinking. I get a bit fucking arsey in that situation, and I really hate it if we get to a hotel and checking in takes forever.

FRED: It's the same with tour managers. Having been on the road since 1978, we know what a good tour manager looks like, and we get annoyed if they don't control the situation.

RICH: Because the situation then controls us, and that's very irritating.

FRED: We earned a lot of money early on, but once we went independent in 1994, we started haemorrhaging money – so we made a lot and then we spent a lot. But we have no regrets. Regrets don't really take you anywhere, do they? The only thing you can do is learn from your mistakes.

RICH: Anyway, I think if the second album had taken off, it would have been a different story. The pressure would have made us unbearable.

FRED: I'd be in rehab.

RICH: Me too, probably. When the band got big, the weird thing was that we lost as many friends as we made. Some people we knew were insanely jealous. They couldn't handle it, especially some musician friends.

FRED: We also lost contact with people, which is inevitable when we were touring so much.

RICH: Mum was very proud of our success. She supported what we were doing. We often took her to TV shows and other events – she loved that. We paid for her to go to Canada to see an old school friend, and she was so excited.

FRED: There were lots of good things about being successful, despite all the complaining we're doing in this chapter.

RICH: Our success was tempered by the fact that we didn't have a band. We hadn't grown up with a bunch of musicians in a tight unit and gone off and played Red Rocks or whatever. It was a different feeling, somehow.

FRED: By 1994 we were just tired, and we didn't give a shit. We were done with the idea of working with Tug, and the relationship with Rob wasn't what it had been either. What would have been really cool would be to do an interim single with someone famous. That would have kept the momentum going.

RICH: Before we could fuck off and be independent, Tug still had an option for a third album from us.

FRED: They didn't want it, though. I have a copy of an internal memo within Tug that said, 'Regarding Right Said Fred's third option, their position is weak in the marketplace and I suggest we kick them while they're down.' Nice.

RICH: This is from a company who had become multi-millionaires by setting up a record label totally on our backs.

FRED: They didn't exercise that option, obviously, but at the same time, we were keen to get away from them, so we were being deliberately difficult.

RICH: We were quite arsey at times, I admit. Everybody in the business can spread their risk but artists can't. All the artist has is themselves.

FRED: I'll say right here and now that I take my share of responsibility for being hard to work with. At this point, I was probably being too much of a party boy: I buried myself in an alternative lifestyle.

RICH: Yes, we weren't always the easiest to work with. One problem was that you and I both have a sense of humour which nobody else gets. For example, as part of our merch a few years ago we had a girls' T-shirt that read 'Piss off, I'm on the blob'. Nobody liked it… we loved it.

FRED: We had to present *Top of the Pops* in Germany and Stephen Gately of Boyzone was on. He had a stutter, so I said, 'Here's Stephen G-G-Gately,' and they went fucking mental. I thought it was funny. Fortunately it was a pre-record, not live.

RICH: So we left Tug Records in 1995. We believe one of the biggest factors in our downfall while signed to them was that no one in the team had specific experience. You, me and Rob weren't a band, we were a songwriting partnership. Tamzin had never been a manager and Tug Records had never been a record label. It was inevitable the wheels would come off sooner rather than later.

FRED: We fell out with them pretty badly, it has to be said. A car belonging to someone at the label got attacked with acid, and they said it was us. Of course, it wasn't, so we said, 'Prove it, and by the way, you have no idea how many of your artists hate you.' They said, 'We'll forget this whole matter if you give £5,000 to our favourite charity.' We didn't.

RICH: You've got to have the courage to walk away from these toxic situations. You're dazzled by it all at the beginning, so you make all sorts of mistakes – and after a while, desperation oozes out of every pore. You've got to have the strength to say no.

FRED: We set up our own record label in 1994, and we called it Happy Valley, because that was when I started taking antidepressants.

RICH: We both suffer from depression, but we generally manage it all right.

FRED: I know when it's coming, because I feel tired, tearful, disconnected and angry, and I have the compulsion to eat a lot. Comfort food, I guess. I tend to be in bed a lot on those days.

RICH: Maybe it's a seasonal thing, the way we feel about life. You know, you have summer times and winter times.

FRED: Going indie was challenging for lots of reasons, because we weren't a band, and we had no specific sound. Also, at this point in the mid-nineties in the UK, Britpop was inescapable, which meant that the landscape was difficult for us.

RICH: I didn't like Britpop. Regurgitated sixties melodies don't do much for me.

FRED: Same here, although I did like the Seattle scene. It made Britpop sound very stale.

RICH: The Spice Girls were just about to break at the time. Do you remember when we shared a green room with them in Belgium, and they were very nervous?

FRED: They seemed very much under the record label's thumb.

RICH: Anyway, running our own operation was the obvious thing to do. Remember, we'd been managing ourselves for ten years before anyone ever heard of us.

FRED: When we set Happy Valley Records up, Sony were interested in signing us, but we were keen on the idea of having our own label and licensing the material out. If Happy Valley had been managed properly, it could have been a very lucrative model.

RICH: By now we were being managed by Jazz Summers, who had a history with Wham! and other bands. We worked with him when we did our third album, *Smashing!*.

FRED: Our agent at the time said, 'Despite all his faults, I think Jazz Summers could be the guy for you.'

RICH: That turned out to be a huge error, because he wasn't the guy for us at all.

FRED: I remember Jazz was very good at meetings – he always took control of the room. He had a healthy disrespect for people, so he'd say, 'This is the way it's going to work.'

RICH: To begin with, I quite liked Jazz, because he came to the studio and he got involved in the tracks. But the minute the first single didn't leap into the Top 10, he lost interest, because his view was that a pop band is only as good as its last hit.

FRED: He also ripped us off for a huge amount of money. He did this by frontloading the deal, which meant that he was taking a commission from costs such as videos and travel, rather than incoming revenue. We were being paid a lot of money from overseas territories for the new album, but not only was he spending parts of that money which should have been held back for us, he was taking a commission off things that were never commissionable.

RICH: It was completely dishonest.

FRED: Jazz also ripped us off by not using the deal money to supply the stores with our albums when we did in-store appearances. Sadly, our lawyers were asleep at the wheel, so we had to go back later and renegotiate these deals retrospectively, which cost us a fortune.

RICH: We were coming back from Mauritius once, after a very chilled three-week holiday, and we went into the business lounge – and who should be sitting there? Jazz Summers, in a linen suit. He had obviously been there on holiday at the same time as us. We knew he owed us a shitload of money, so the minute I saw this bastard, I saw red. Right in front of everybody in that lounge, I grabbed him and shouted, 'You ripped us off! How the fuck do you live with yourself?'

FRED: He didn't really have much to say to that.

RICH: No, it wasn't a very illuminating conversation. What was insane about that is that it was meant to be a chilled-out holiday. Anyway, we don't generally get physical.

FRED: Do you remember that time when some yob was giving me grief once, and because he had tons of spots, I called him 'pizza face'. He was so angry, because his friends fell about laughing at that. I woke up the next morning and he had covered my entire car in dog shit. Literally, the entire car. Fortunately, it was just a hire car, so I took it to the carwash and that was it, but to this day I wonder where he got hold of that much dog shit.

RICH: He must have been quite resourceful. Anyway, Jazz took our money. A lot of it.

FRED: We never got what we were owed.

RICH: We knew we'd never get it, and indeed we never did, because Jazz died in 2015.

FRED: Life's too short to carry this negativity around, but even so, I can hold a grudge for ages.

RICH: It's different for me. I don't think about it from one year to the next. I think you have more of a long-term grudge for these people than I do.

FRED: I do. Someone once told me, 'Forgive but don't forget.' That's pretty much how I live, because if you don't forgive, you will be pissed off forever, but at the same time, never forget what happened or it will happen again.

RICH: I think that if you make the decision to steal someone's money, you should be responsible for the outcome. You've made that decision, and that's fine because you're an adult, but don't be surprised if that decision comes back and bites you in the face, which it always will.

FRED: There was a guy who worked with Jazz, and we were talking about doing some business that involved a lot of our money, so as a joke I said, 'Don't make me come up to the office with my baseball bat,' but he was terrified and he started calling people to ask if I was serious.

RICH: All these slimy people seem to know each other, so you just go from one slimy setup to another. We didn't seem to be able to break that pattern.

FRED: One of the people who was very good at making us wake up and get our shit together was Neil Warnock, a booking agent who managed us for a short time. He was a good guy, very no-nonsense, and he worked very hard for us and was supportive. Neil came to a club gig we were doing, but it was poorly attended so we drank too much and generally fucked around. Afterwards Neil lost his mind with us: he said, 'Be professional. Every gig is as important as the next. Whether it's ten people or ten thousand, they've paid for a show.' He was 100 per cent right.

RICH: In 1994, we played in South Africa, and apparently we were the first white artists to appear there after Nelson Mandela's election as president. He wanted to invite two bands from overseas, so he invited Arrested Development and us, so we went over. Did he personally know our music? Fuck knows.

FRED: That was an amazing trip, though.

RICH: I was struck by the warmth of the South Africans that we met, particularly in Soweto – they were fantastic people – and we were struck by the size of Soweto itself. People in the West don't realise how huge it is. When we got there, a whole bunch of local musicians sang a version of 'I'm Too Sexy' for us, with African percussion and beautiful South African harmonies. Sadly, nobody filmed it.

FRED: We were humbled and honoured to be part of it.

RICH: I remember the phone ringing in the car as we drove to Johannesburg. The driver said, 'It's the British Embassy,' which I thought was fantastic, because only important people get that kind of call. Surely it had to be Nelson himself? But no, it turned out that my landlady in London, who worked in the South African consulate, was pissed off because we owed her money for a gas bill.

FRED: In 1996, we released *Smashing!* on Happy Valley. Some of the songs on that album were pretty good, I think. 'Big Time' did well and so did 'Living on a Dream'. We spent too much on the album, though. I know that I slag off record labels, but my heart also goes out to them because we became a record label ourselves, and it's a fucking tough gig.

RICH: After the album came out we went on the road, and it was quite a successful run. Rob was on some of those tours, but not all the time, so we got dep guitarists in. We had a really good backing singer called Dawn Knight who had a unique voice. She was really good fun to tour with. When we were landing in South Africa, she stared out of the window and said, 'Where's the jungles?'

FRED: Brilliant! She was great, although you can't say that about everyone we met at the time. I remember we did a gig in 1996 in Germany with an American heavy metal band, and they slagged us off during soundcheck, saying, 'They're a bit too fucking gay for our tastes.' They didn't realise Craig Duffy, our tour manager, was there watching the soundcheck.

RICH: After that they wanted to share our dressing room, but we told them to go and fuck themselves.

FRED: Rob left the band after *Smashing!*, probably around 1997. It was a mutual agreement to knock it on the head. We sat down with our accountant and we were looking at business options, and it was going to be financially beneficial for all of us if we dissolved one of our companies, which was how he left the band.

RICH: It was fun with Rob at first, but he distanced himself through *Sex and Travel* and *Smashing!*, so him not being there after 1997 wasn't such a big deal.

FRED: Rob started hanging out a lot with other artists, which was fine, but then he wouldn't turn up at rehearsals. The last straw came when we were about to tour Europe, but seemingly Rob couldn't be arsed, so we got another guitarist.

RICH: We wished him all the best, despite feeling he'd let us down.

FRED: It also made sense for him to leave because people were still finding it too difficult to accept a band with two bald guys and one with hair. It was too complicated for them. I'm quite serious about that.

RICH: With just two of us in the band, we didn't have to have discussions about our direction any more. It had always been a bit of an issue when Rob was there, so from that point of view, it was easier.

FRED: Do you think Rob might have been embarrassed by being in Right Said Fred?

RICH: I don't know.

FRED: He didn't seem embarrassed by the royalties, though.

RICH: Talking of being embarrassed, or not as the case may be, I embarked on a glittering TV career around this time. From 1996, I was often on *Never Mind the Buzzcocks* – once that year and again in '97 and '98. It was a fun gig to do. I quite enjoyed it.

FRED: You used to have a bit of banter with the presenter Mark Lamarr, which I always thought was funny.

RICH: I remember I said something like, 'I don't like the way that guy's dressed,' and Mark said, 'This isn't *Queer Eye for the Straight Guy.*' He introduced me once by saying, 'As we all know, Richard likes a bit of weight training, but he's never shown any interest in the snatch.' Billy Bragg was also on the show, and he was furious on my behalf – he couldn't understand why I wasn't offended.

FRED: Isn't he offended by everything?

RICH: Another thing that I did was co-present a late-night TV show called *Gaytime TV* with Rhona Cameron. I liked working with Rhona, but unfortunately it proved to be very difficult attracting artists to appear on a 'gay' show – even gay artists wouldn't come on the show. It always felt to me that there was a stressful situation going on in the background, because the BBC knew that it was part of its remit to provide this kind of programming, but at the same time it wasn't drawing the kind of ratings that they needed. At one point they brought in another producer to try and jazz it up, but that didn't really work. Still, I did it for four years, all the way up to 1999, so it can't have been a complete disaster.

FRED: I came on set a few times; I thought it was a good show.

RICH: It was at times. There was a boy band that came on called A1, and I said to them, 'Why have you named yourselves after a secondary road?'

FRED: Did they get the joke?

RICH: No.

FRED: Do you think the show served an actual purpose?

RICH: Well, arguably. People were phoning in with coming-out stories, and sending in emails, so they told me to read out the emails when they came in. I was more interested in hearing from people who were going through trouble while coming out, though. That was much more interesting to me, but I wasn't allowed to read any of those out. Taking Phillip Schofield as an example, I think it's an opportunity lost – he could have been very supportive to so many people.

FRED: We are naturally outspoken and we don't like being filtered. To us, this makes a lot of TV very beige and dull.

RICH: In the eighties, a mate of ours was doing sound for Tina Turner, about the time she had a hit with Bryan Adams, so I went down to her soundcheck to see what was going on, and then two stand-ins came on for Bryan and Tina and said, 'Can we rehearse the ad-libs?' That said, it was a great show – but rehearsed ad-libs are not for us.

FRED: We spent a lot of time on tour around this time, including some dates in Japan. The Japanese are lovely people, but it's a very strange country. They didn't have any security at our hotel, so the fans were all sitting in the corridors outside our rooms, waiting for us to come out. We couldn't go out independently: we had to have a security guy follow us everywhere, which drove me nuts.

RICH: A lot of the Japanese girls would make these little home-made cards and posters for us. Quite often they'd be very flowery, with hearts and everything, and there would be a love poem written around the edge. In the middle, in large letters, it would say 'Fuck me, please'. It was really odd.

FRED: It wasn't all plain sailing, of course. You and I actually had a fight when we were in Munich in 1996.

RICH: Did we? What was it about?

FRED: Basically the same, long-standing thing that has always annoyed me about you – which is that when something is wrong, you just complain about it rather than talking to the actual person who can solve it. I always say, 'Don't have a go at me. Talk to the person who is responsible.'

RICH: Ah yes – that!

FRED: We were on a boy-band tour in Europe, which was completely ridiculous. While we were in the lift, you started whining about being on the tour and implying that I should speak to our manager. We'd been drinking, and we started having a go at each other, and I said, 'Don't fucking talk to me, talk to them!' and it came to blows. At each floor the door opened, but no one wanted to get in with two slapheads knocking seven bells out of each other. Craig Duffy had to hold us apart. It was funny, because we didn't fight when we were kids.

RICH: I did push you in a pond once.

FRED: So you did.

RICH: I'm sure you deserved it. Look, the mid-nineties were stressful. I had an operation on my left knee around this time. I fell off a stage when we were doing a video and that, coupled with doing leg extensions at the gym, which are really bad for your knees, meant that my left knee had lost its cartilage. It's very clever how they fix it. They drill holes into the back of the kneecap – really shallow ones that don't go all the way through – so the blood floods in and solidifies, and that makes the kneecap stronger. It's not as good as it was before, but it's much better than having a replacement.

FRED: From '98 to 2000 we reduced our workload for many reasons. Richard's partner Stuart was in very poor health, Mum's boyfriend had recently died, my depression was becoming a real issue, and to be honest we were happy to take time out. Offers were still frequent: we were even asked to do Eurovision a few times, both as songwriters and as performers, but we were never tempted. It would have been the kiss of death in our opinion.

RICH: I'd do it as a writer.

FRED: Me too, but we wouldn't be able to write what you wanted to write.

RICH: The only similar thing I would probably do now is be on the panel of one of those reality shows like *The Voice*, provided I was allowed to say what I actually thought. That would be quite good.

FRED: Seriously? Do you think you you'd enjoy that?

RICH: Maybe. On another note, do you remember the centre-fold we did for German *Playgirl* in about 1997?

FRED: Yes, indeed I do!

RICH: It paid a lot of money. We look a weird kind of orange-brown in the pictures. We'd taken advice from a professional

115

bodybuilder, who said that if you drink cherry brandy before you do a shoot, it will tint your sweat. Our mistake was to drink way too much and we got very drunk.

FRED: At this point our income went up significantly while our careers were flatlining, and what this taught us very quickly is that song usage is key. Say your track is the lead song in *Beverly Hills, 90210* or *Westworld*, and all you've done is send them an audio file while sitting at home, that's a great position to be in. Suddenly, you think, 'Hang about, we've got this song on that movie, which is all over the world, and we haven't had to leave our front room!'

RICH: That was a massive eye-opener – there's a whole world of music beyond being in the charts.

FRED: So let's talk about the good times for a bit. Have you got any weird and wonderful stories to share?

RICH: Oh, I'm sure we can think of some...

You're My Mate
Fairbrass/Fairbrass/Gray (2001)
Reprinted with permission from FAR Songs

I'll tell you what I think, I think she's a cow
She's let you down too many times now
Let's go for a drink, forget it for now
Put it behind you, I think it's your round

Cos you're my mate and I will stand by you
You're my mate and I will stand by you
And in the face of things that could hurt you
You're my mate and I will stand by you

I'll tell you what I think, I think he's a pain
He ain't got a car but he drives you insane
Let's go for a drink and sink a few
Enough about him, let's talk about you

Cos you're my mate and I will stand by you
All I wanna do is get drunk here with you
Cos you're my mate and I will stand by you
Cos you're my mate

Taxi!

FRED: This song was inspired by my divorce from my first wife, and sitting down and talking my way through it with you. The 'cow' in the song is not my ex-wife Louise, though: I should make that clear.

RICH: We performed that song at a gig in the UK, and a reviewer wrote: '"You're My Mate" is one of the worst songs ever recorded. However, the crowd seemed to like it.'

FRED: It's about friendship – just looking after each other.

RICH: We had the middle eight line 'All I wanna do is get drunk here with you' first, and slotted it into the song when it took shape.

FRED: The 'Taxi!' at the end comes from a video that we shot but didn't use. It stayed in the song as a hangover from that video.

Mum and Dad, Brighton seafront, early 1950's.

Fred and Rich circa 1964.

Mum at the back, Fred, Dad, Rich, dog Chloe, taken at home circa 1961.

Lead guitarist Mike Gerrard.   Bass player Richard Fairbrass.   Vocalist Fred Fairbrass.   Drummer Tommy O'Donnell.

Ronnie Scott's encores the hard working Actors

WITH FIFTEEN gigs fixed up in the next few

people present was a sight even this popular rock spot

Farm, Lingfield, plays lead guitar and co-writes their

fidently claim it is original enough not to need a label.

East Grinstead Observer, our local newspaper, October 1977.

EAST GRINSTEAD OBSERVER

Richard and Fred in the back garden at home, early seventies.

Factory gig poster, July 1978.

Mike Gerrard at the back, (L-R) Tommy O'Donnell, Richard, Fred. Rehearsal in a converted barn, 1977.

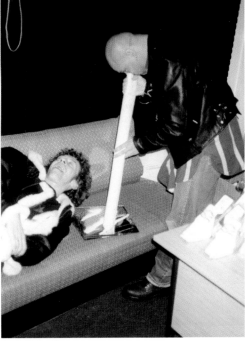

1st PA performance of 'I'm Too Sexy', somewhere in Essex, June 1991.

Fake Coke on tour, 1995.

Fred and Rich, early promo shot.
JOHN STODDART/POPPERFOTO

Rob Manzoli, Peter Cook, Rich and
Fred in front, Red Nose Day, 1993.
COMIC RELIEF/GETTY IMAGES

Radio 1 Road Show, 1991.
PICTORIAL PRESS LTD/ALAMY

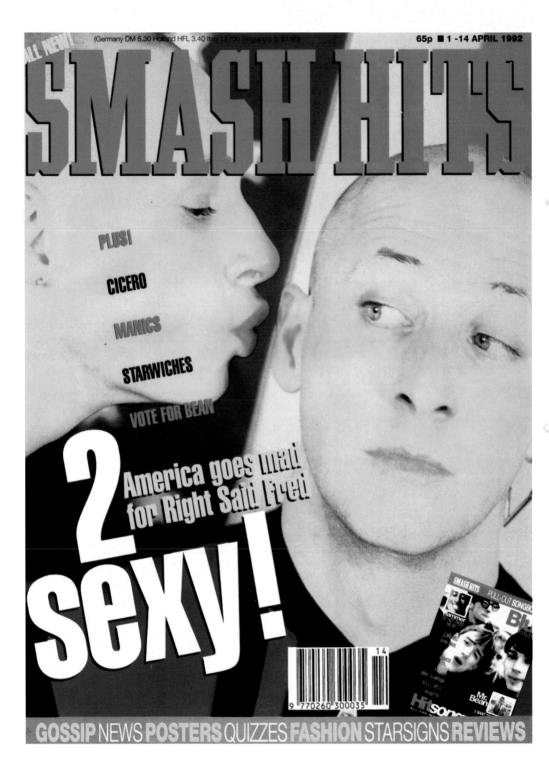

Smash Hits, 1992.
SMASH HITS

On the road in the UK, 2017.
JULES ANNAN/ALAMY

Fred's daughter Marina and her fiancé, Scott.

Alex, Fred's wife.

Rich and Stuart, Christmas in Mauritius, 1997.

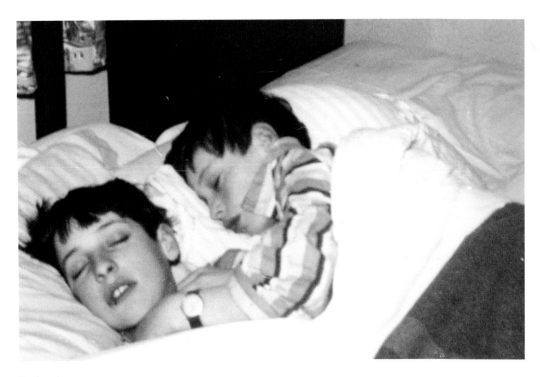

Brothers in arms.

Chapter 5

Muscles, Drugs and Fucking

Everything you ever wanted to know about bodily matters.

RICH: In 1987, I was walking past a shop window that had reflective stuff on it, like a big mirror. I walked past and I realised that I looked like a bloody Afghan hound. I had long hair and a big fucking nose, and I thought, 'I'm not going to look like that any more.' I was really skinny, so I just thought, 'Right, let's get down the gym.' That's where weight training started. After a while you came down as well.

FRED: When I first went, I thought, 'I'm not sure about this,' and then a couple of days later, I started to enjoy the atmosphere and the people and the camaraderie.

RICH: The gym is time just for you. It's a little bit like smoking. That's the one great thing I miss about smoking. When you stand outside on the doorstep and have a cigarette, it's just your time. I stopped about ten years ago after Stuart died.

FRED: We ended up running a gym in Putney, south-west London, and then the band took off.

RICH: We trained a lot of people at that gym, and what I liked about that was that sometimes you get someone who really gets the training bug, and over a year, you see them change. People suddenly gain discipline and self-esteem, and they change the way they dress. Quite often their partners will change along the way too.

FRED: I really liked personal training; it's quite an intimate experience.

RICH: After a while we experimented with steroids. A guy at the gym used to inject us in the arse, but then we limited ourselves to tablets. They're a shortcut to building muscle mass: you can make the same gains without them, but you have to work twice as hard for twice as long.

FRED: As with everything else, you can buy dodgy stuff, so we were very careful.

RICH: I wouldn't recommend steroids, really. If you want to do them, make absolutely sure you trust your supplier, and be aware that they can be addictive, not chemically but psychologically. When you get really big, you don't want to stop – you want to keep doing them.

FRED: You put on muscle faster than I do. I have to work harder.

RICH: I got pretty serious about it.

FRED: Yeah, me too. I would get up in the morning at about four and eat a yam, because it's a slow-release carbohydrate, and then I'd go back to bed. We worked really hard. Even when we went on the road, we used to make sure that we had time for training.

RICH: Loads of people have caffeine before they train. In fact, that's the standard procedure – drink an espresso and go to the gym.

FRED: I used to train for the physical gains, but now I train for my physical and mental wellbeing.

RICH: I got quite addicted to the idea of getting big, but at the same time, we weren't meatheads. You need to look fit on stage, but not lumbering or cumbersome, which can happen if you put on too much muscle.

FRED: Nowadays, we still train but we're more focused on good mental health.

RICH: I like the gym lifestyle. A lot of people in the gym are very supportive, like-minded people: we swap ideas about training and so on. I got into the science, and I started reading about the slow-twitch muscle, the fast-twitch muscle and all that stuff.

FRED: I had a tummy tuck in 2004 after being ill and putting on some weight. I'd gained a bit of fat, mostly around the middle, and I could not shift it for love nor money. I went to see my doctor, and he said, 'Look, other doctors will say do this and do that, but in my honest opinion, you are not going to get rid of that fat without having it sucked out.' So I went to a clinic in London to have it done, but unfortunately, I picked the wrong doctor to do it. Although he took out around seven pounds of fat, he left the skin damaged. I've got a nasty scar on my stomach. The other thing that freaked me out was that the bruising from the operation turned my cock and balls completely black for a while. That really freaked me out!

RICH: Yes, that must have been quite a shock.

FRED: It would have been nice to have been told that in advance. These clinics are surreal, by the way. My wife worked at one where a Saudi Arabian princess came over and paid 150,000 euros to have her jaw moved a millimetre forward. These people have too much time on their hands.

RICH: Like most bands we've enjoyed a stimulating drug or two in our time. When we first moved to London, we didn't have any money, so speed was the drug of choice.

FRED: I used to sell speed and coke, as I mentioned before. I was a minicab driver in Fulham in 1982, and I used to work nights, and a bloke in the house I was living in was an amphetamine cook. So I used to buy a couple of grammes here and there, firstly to keep awake, but then I had customers that wanted to buy it. I could deal in the car.

121

RICH: One of our friends used to put speed in milk and drink it first thing in the mornings. I never did that myself. I didn't like anything that made me feel like I was losing control, which is why I liked coke, because you never feel like that. I don't like too much booze for the same reason, because I don't like feeling that I'm losing my grip on things.

FRED: I did GHB once, which you're supposed to sip slowly from a glass of water to get a mild buzz – but because I was coked off my head at the time, I was thirsty, so I drank it all in one go. Someone said, 'Where's that glass?' and I said I'd drunk it. He said, 'You fucking idiot!' I tried it on with one of the blokes I was with, because I was so off my head I couldn't tell if he was male or female. Then I collapsed on a bed and slept for six hours.

RICH: You know how you can sniff the fumes from vodka and they make you intoxicated? You sniffed the actual vodka once.

FRED: We were in Belgium waiting to do a TV show, and half my face was paralysed. I had to do an interview with half my face motionless. People were probably saying that the bloke from Right Said Fred doesn't look too clever.

RICH: In our experience the music business doesn't mind the use of coke. Artists can function on it.

FRED: It's not like meth or heroin, where the user can be impossible to work with.

RICH: When you're young, you can do coke one night and the next day you feel fine. But if I did it now, it would take me two or three days to get over it.

FRED: I did a speedball once, which is a mix of coke and smack. You snort it, and you get this weird sense of calm and a buzz at the same time, but I can't really recommend it. I was a fan of ecstasy for a while.

122

RICH: Definitely, but the weird thing about ecstasy is trying to repeat the first one. The first one can be fucking brilliant but the second one is always disappointing.

FRED: I used to put MDMA in champagne. That was fun, because the bubbles go into your bloodstream much quicker and they take the drug with them, so you get this big hit. I did acid a few times too – we had a lot of fun with that.

RICH: Oh yeah. I did it once and it just made me giggle. Everything was funny.

FRED: Do you remember when I pissed my pants on acid? I thought it was the funniest thing in the world. We got the munchies at about 3 a.m. and went to our local 24-hour garage for chocolate. The lady wouldn't serve us and called the police. For some reason I thought that was hilarious. Anything else?

RICH: I used to like poppers, although they can give me a blinding headache. They're good for sex because they make you very horny. It dilates the blood vessels, apparently. You often see gay guys on the dancefloor with a bottle permanently stuck up their nose. They've banned pure amyl nitrate, although now you can buy a synthetic version that is nowhere near as good. They always ban the fun stuff.

FRED: I drank a bit on our early tours. I didn't like getting stoned, but the minute I took coke, I really liked it. That was in my mid-twenties. We were living in Putney and we got to know a guy who had been signed as the UK's version of Bruce Springsteen. To supplement his lifestyle he was dealing coke, and because we were all friends we used to sit up with him and play a lot of poker and do a lot of gear, and we didn't have to pay for it because he was a mate.

RICH: He got busted and had to go clean, I remember.

FRED: He did. I only did a couple of lines of coke here and there back then, but once I had money in my pocket and I was cash-rich, I used to do quite a lot. I got into it really heavily in the mid-nineties on a daily basis. I wouldn't leave the house without it. I didn't like people who didn't do it, so all my friends were of the same mindset. I liked the lifestyle.

RICH: You were more into coke than I was.

FRED: I suppose I was a heavy user, but I wasn't addicted to it. I didn't wake up and need it – I'd just wake up and look forward to it. And when I had to stop, I just did it. No rehab.

RICH: If it wasn't for the comedown afterwards, and the way it fucks your body up, I'd still do it. But as you get older, the comedown is worse, and we're both quite vain, so doing anything that's bad for your skin or bad for the way you look isn't a priority. Getting a good night's sleep is important for me, as well.

FRED: Me too, because the next day after coke can be terrible. I think it affected my mental health, actually, and in 2003 I thought it had damaged my physical health too. You found me collapsed in my home and I was rushed to hospital. The doctors thought I had something called cocaine heart, which is when the back of your heart beats so violently that it bruises, but what I actually had was a severe lung infection. It was very serious for a while, and they told you to expect the worst.

RICH: They actually gave you only three or four hours to live.

FRED: Later, the doctor told me that my weight training had saved my life. My basic constitution is really strong. When I spoke to the consultant during convalescence, I was honest with him and I said, 'How much of this is due to drugs? I play in a band, we've been partying a lot with coke and there's a lot of sleep deprivation.' And he said, 'There's no visible cocaine damage. I shouldn't really tell you that, but that's the truth.'

RICH: When we were on the road, we mainly used coke just to keep us up, because we had a heavy schedule. We were tired a lot of the time, maybe because our band broke late. We weren't 20, we were in our mid-thirties.

FRED: We've been very frank in lots of interviews about our drug use and steroid use, but they always take it out.

RICH: The thing about coke is you think you're really fucking happening, but then you catch sight of yourself in the mirror and you think, 'Oh my God.' Veins pumping, eyes bulging, and completely incapable of getting a hard-on. Talking of which, let's talk about shagging for a bit.

FRED: When was your first shag? Was it that girl at that public school you were seeing when you were about 16 or something?

RICH: Ah, Jane. She was about to finish school, and said, 'It's my last night. Will you come over?' She was a prefect at this school, so she had her own room. I thought, 'Brilliant! Time for my first shag!' and went over there. We were about to go for it – but she suddenly said, 'I can't do this.' So I had to sleep on the floor. Her parents came the next morning to pick her up and take her back home. I still remember the look her father gave me. I wanted to say to him, 'Don't look at me like that. I didn't do anything!' In the end, my first time was with a girl from college. I didn't have meaningful sex until I was about 25 years old, unless you include random fumblings. That's not because there was any trauma or anything weird in my background. I just think that penetrating somebody is significant, and you shouldn't do it unless it means something.

FRED: Still, 25 is a bit late for your first shag.

RICH: I guess I was a late bloomer.

FRED: Ha ha! You think?

RICH: Oh, I don't know. I've never really given this any thought. I suppose I don't want to fuck anyone I don't really care about. I don't like the idea of just fucking somebody for the sake of it, generally anyway.

FRED: Not much like me then.

RICH: In late 1991, we were doing a PA in Cardiff, and after the show, I started mingling with the crowd and I picked up this girl who was maybe 18 or 19 years old. We decided to go back to my hotel room, but she said, 'I can't go without my mum.' I said, 'Er, well, okay then.' This was the night that Freddie Mercury died, and we all watched the news on the TV in my room. It was me, the mum and the daughter, just lying on the bed. I know what you're thinking, but no, nothing happened. It was very bizarre.

FRED: We tend to say what we think about gender politics, but we don't get too embroiled in it, because if you're not careful you become irrevocably associated with it and suddenly that's all you are. For us, music is still the most important thing, so we're very mindful of not doing too much of that. Whenever we get called equal rights activists, I think that's a bit rude to real activists.

RICH: Funnily enough, I have never received an invitation to any HIV fundraisers or gay-focused events, despite being in a relationship with Stuart for twenty-eight years, coming out in 1991, and him being HIV positive for twenty-seven of those years.

FRED: Well, we never made a big deal about you being gay or not gay, did we?

RICH: Not really. When anybody asked me about it, I used to say I was bisexual, which made sense then because I did have girlfriends. But I remember reading what Graham Chapman said about this. He said he had to decide one day whether he was gay or straight, and he was thinking, 'If I fancy more men than women on this bus, then I must be gay,' and that was how he did it. I did it too, so I don't define myself as bisexual so much these days. I'm probably about 30 per cent straight, if I was pushed to come up with a number.

FRED: A 70/30 split seems about right in your case, I'd say.

RICH: I say that because I'm a bit more relaxed about the idea of sexual performance when I'm with a man. I feel that a performance is more expected of you when you're with a woman.

FRED: The same basic stuff gets done in both cases, though.

RICH: That's a pretty romantic way of putting it.

FRED: Yes. My wife's a lucky lady.

RICH: There's an image that for gay guys, sex is all about fucking, but you know, that's never been a big part of my life. For me, sex with a man is more about a mental connection. I'd love to be one of these people who can just sleep around, but I've never been able to do it unless I actually like the person I'm with. I want to talk about life with them. The actual penetration has never been my main objective.

FRED: Ooh, you're so deep.

RICH: I've got to know a few escorts, male and female, over the years. They're interesting people, but sometimes quite damaged, psychologically. There's a guy I know, who is physically skinny, but he's in demand among men that want to get fucked by a guy with a big cock. I think, deep down, he just wants to be looked after. Don't we all want that, really? As humans, we like to be safe.

FRED: Safe, and also loved. You came out around the time 'Sexy' was released, if I remember correctly.

RICH: Yes, which would have been when I was around 37. Coming out is a fucking difficult thing, so people have to do it at their own pace. At the same time, people put themselves through a lot of pain by trying to dodge the obvious truth. You never know what's going on with people's private lives. Take George Michael, for example – he may have had family issues. No one knows what the personal dynamics are. This makes me tolerant when people don't come out. You have to give them room.

FRED: Personally, I was shocked by the amount of girls who would sleep with me because I was famous. Some of the girls were probably looking for a relationship; for others, perhaps it was a rite of passage. I think we both used each other. Sex on the road is very opportunistic.

RICH: It was the nature of how we sold ourselves. It was physical. It was sexual. Because the image of our band was very different to that of other bands, they expected us to be more fun to be with, but they were often disappointed.

FRED: It wasn't always fun. Sometimes it was scary. I remember a stripper invited me back to her place, and she had a security camera outside her house and a screen on her bedroom wall that showed you what was happening outside. She looked at the screen and got really panicky, because she could see all these flames: an admirer had leaned a wooden pallet against her front door and set it on fire.

RICH: That's one way of breaking up with someone.

FRED: After visiting a strip club in Texas I invited a girl back to my hotel room for a drink, then two or three of her friends also tagged along, and then we picked up some other girls on the way. So I had seven girls in my room. Sadly, one of the girls had been beaten up by her boyfriend and was very upset, so I went from being this pop star who is about to have a massive orgy to being a kind of sympathetic counsellor, because they all started sharing their stories of disappointment and loss and abuse. The room service staff would come in and take a look at me and these seven girls, all of whom were crying, and they were clearly thinking, 'What the fuck is going on in here?' We sat up till dawn and my room service bill was in the thousands... that said, the girls were lovely.

RICH: Do you remember when we picked up our first two groupies in about 1977? We were driving home with them, then suddenly we had to brake sharply. There were no seat belts, so one of them flew off the front seat and hit the windscreen. When she got home she passed out and ended up in a coma. Our first foray into the world of groupies and this poor girl ends up in a coma. That's very Right Said Fred.

FRED: Fortunately she recovered.

RICH: We had to get used to the idea of our bodies being public property. I did a nude photoshoot once, and it was extremely cold in the room... that's my excuse anyway. The photos appeared in a magazine, and at one of our gigs, all these women in the front row were holding up the photos from the magazine. That was embarrassing and funny in equal measure.

FRED: We used to get groped a lot, by both men and women, even before the band was famous.

RICH: Yeah, I got groped once by a famous A&R guy in New York in 1987 at the Limelight club. He put his hand on my crotch and said, 'Are we going to do this?', implying that a record deal would be in the offing if I came across. I didn't come across, so no deal. To be honest I didn't particularly mind – it comes with the territory.

FRED: The casting couch is centuries old.

RICH: Around 1984, we were involved in an HIV charity benefit concert. Ronnie Barker was the host, and one of the producers, who was present when we rehearsed, was the broadcaster Ned Sherrin. You and I were dressed as scouts, and halfway through rehearsals, Ned came up to us and said, 'Do you fancy coming over for dinner?' We thought, 'Well, he's famous, and we've seen him on TV, so let's go. It might be quite useful.' We also thought that hanging out with people like Ned Sherrin would help us get an Equity card. Anyway, the day before the dinner, you said, 'I'm not going.' I thought it would be rude to cancel at the last minute, so I went on my own. I get there, and he's made chicken for dinner, and we're sitting at either end of a long table. With no preamble whatsoever, he suddenly said, 'I have a small penis and I like to get fucked.' At that point I did the English thing and pretended I hadn't heard what he said. Then we moved into the front room and he put a video on of two naked boys wrestling on a mat. He went off to make tea while I sat on the sofa. He then came in with the tea and sat right next to me. There were many sofas he could have chosen, but he decided to sit right next to me, and he put his hand on my crotch. I stood up and said, 'Ned, this is not going to happen, so forget it.' He said, 'Well, I'm going to have a wank,' and started to do just that. All I could hear was the sofa squeaking. Then he threw me out. Many years later, I met him on his BBC radio show, *Loose Ends*, after the band broke. He didn't refer to it at all – he just greeted me in the usual manner.

FRED: After the band broke I was the token straight bloke. People knew that you were gay, our stylist was gay, our make-up guy was gay and the record company rep was gay, so there was a bottleneck when it came to female groupies.

RICH: You were a trooper, though, and gave it your best shot.

FRED: I did, but I got bored with having sex, because it was so easy. 'I'm Too Sexy' was so huge, and we were on every TV show and magazine cover, so anywhere you went you could just click your fingers and a girl would be there. After the initial novelty wore off, I started thinking, 'It would be really nice to sit around and talk with someone.'

RICH: Discussing the national debt after a show can be a buzzkill, though.

FRED: I remember going to a party in Tokyo, and I came back to my hotel room with a girl called Amber. I think she was an

American model – a pretty good-looking lady. Anyway, we had sex and I nodded off. When I woke up, she was getting dressed and was on the phone, saying, 'Mom, I just fucked the guy from Right Said Fred!'

RICH: A truly heartwarming story.

FRED: We used to get invited to what were called 'suck and fuck' parties, a kind of swingers' party for celebrities. You get sucked or fucked, depending on what you want to do. They were very secretive: you had to call all these phone numbers to get certain codes before you found out where they were, although they were always up in the Hollywood Hills. It was very *Eyes Wide Shut*.

RICH: We also got approached by a couple of people in the UK. There's a group of very wealthy businessmen and women who like to party with – and fuck – celebrities. Apparently, our names were high on their list. You can charge a lot of money for this, but we said thanks but no thanks.

FRED: This happened a lot. We were on a boat in the Caribbean once, and these two very large, blinged, middle-aged ladies said, 'If you come to our cabin and take your clothes off, so we can look at your bodies, we'll give you ten grand each.' We considered giving them ten grand each to keep their clothes on.

RICH: I'm not a number, I'm a human being... I said no because I'm quite suspicious of some people. I don't really do the groupie thing. But I do remember there was one guy in Brisbane who had been eyeing me up over dinner. Someone told this guy my room number, so I was lying in bed and there was a knock on the door. I just pretended I wasn't there. It really wasn't my thing.

FRED: You're a bit up your arse sometimes.

RICH: I went with a couple of guys while I was away – literally, just a couple. It was no more than about two or three. One of them was a model, a beautiful guy from Colombia, who I ended up in bed with. It turned out that he had a contract in America to advertise jeans. When we went to LA, we saw pictures of him on these huge fucking posters.

FRED: Guys used to approach you a lot, though, even if you mostly said no. Sometimes I also got included. When we were in Australia, one night after a gig I was signing an autograph bending over a table. Our security guy came up behind me with the biggest hard-on and stuck it right up against my arse. He said to me, 'It'll be nice to hang out later.' I could feel this thing pressing against me and I thought, 'That's not going to happen,' but he was a big bloke, so I just sort of smiled and got on with the autographs.

RICH: And when I did have sex with these people, it wasn't always that good. I remember when I first moved to London, one of my first sexual experiences with a man was with a guy called Brian, an American. I woke up the next morning, and he was lying there, and I remember thinking, 'Well, that was crap. What the fuck was all the fuss about? This is shit.' Anybody would think that gay sex was threatening because it was so brilliant, and this was not.

FRED: I remember that guy. Were you with him for quite a while?

RICH: I was. When Brian first came to the UK, the minute he walked out of Heathrow Airport, he saw this huge ad for faggots, the food, and he thought it was a pro-gay thing. He thought, 'Oh, this is fantastic. This country is so cool' – and then he realised it was advertising a meat dish.

FRED: Oh, that is great.

RICH: We were friends for quite a while, and in the end, he met a guy called Brad and they moved to Alaska. What was weird was that I never heard from him when we got famous in

America. I never heard a single word. Maybe he just moved on. You know, I think for a lot of people, their sexual preference is a badge or something. They have to openly state it, by the way they walk and the way they dress. It's like gay bookshops and gay newspapers and gay films: some people just immerse themselves in it, and I never really have.

FRED: Both of us, professionally and personally, have always lived in the margins.

RICH: I've just started a new relationship. He's a nice guy – a very old soul – and a prostitute. It makes me laugh when I hear people saying, 'I've never paid for sex.' You've paid for sex a million times – when you take someone out for dinner, or if you go into a club and buy someone a drink. I've never had a problem with that. It's never struck me as being weird. I don't go to dating sites, because for a lot of people those sites are just about blow and go, which is not my thing.

FRED: Are you particularly looking for a relationship?

RICH: No. I was in a relationship with Stuart for such a long time, and I don't know why anybody would want to be with me now – truthfully. It would only be because they think I'm a millionaire, or because they think I'm on TV the whole time, or because I'm a famous person or whatever. It's certainly possible that they would like me just for me, but you never know.

FRED: You never do, that's true.

RICH: In the twelve years since my partner Stuart passed away on 20 September 2010, I have to all intents and purposes been single. Falling for a prostitute – as I did in early 2021 – was not something I anticipated, but that's what happened. Before we met, the past had preoccupied me: my years with Stuart seemed to make any future happiness impossible – and yet my strong feelings for this man not only surprised me, they enabled me to see the possibility of a future unfettered by the past: a future of affection and possibly love, who knows? For this I am now and will always be thankful to him.

FRED: Once you're in the public eye or perceived to have money, it's hard to know why people like you.

RICH: I remember the first time I ever went to a backroom, which is a room in a gay club with a tiny dark blue or red lightbulb casting a very muted light. You go in there and you stand around, and eventually somebody interferes with you, or vice versa.

FRED: There was a gig, or maybe a VIP event or something like that, in Austria where a mother brought her 16-year-old daughter backstage to meet us, because the mum thought the daughter was becoming sexually active and she wanted one of us to be the first person to have sex with her.

RICH: The mother explained this to our Austrian representative, who in turn explained it to us.

FRED: We were all sitting there, and it was quite awkward, as you might imagine.

RICH: Then the mum said, pointing at you, 'Why don't you two go off and have a dance?'

FRED: I was quite happy about that because it took me away from this crazy mother. Then the dad turned up, and we thought it was going to kick off because the dad was presumably going to say, 'What the fuck is going on here?' – but it turned out that he was totally on board with all this.

RICH: So we said to our tour manager, 'We need to get out of here. Let's not upset anybody, but we need to leave right now.'

FRED: As the saying goes, we made our excuses and left. In all seriousness, I think these people trusted us. I think they felt their daughter was in good hands.

RICH: It was just because we were famous. There was no other reason. This happened a few times. Seriously, girls would be brought to us as a sort of sexual souvenir. Of course, we always said no and left, because the whole idea was very uncool.

FRED: We got tons of very sexually fuelled fan letters too. I remember someone sent us a home-made porno video that had been filmed in someone's kitchen, by the looks of it. This video arrived at our PR company, who had an office in Kensington. We were sitting there, going through our post, and they'd ordered a Marks & Spencer's takeaway, so we were having quite a nice time, having lunch. So we find this video cassette and put it in the machine, and it starts playing. At first it's blank, but then you hear what sounds like stilettos walking across a wooden floor. The camera pans back, and suddenly there's a guy tied up, with his legs stretched across a wooden worktop and his ball sack on display. This woman walks in and she's got a mask on. She's holding a hammer and a nail, and she grabs the guy's ball sack and nails it to the wooden worktop. At this point we turned the video off.

RICH: It's a good job we weren't eating meatballs.

FRED: It turns out that the skin of a scrotum heals really quickly. I know this because I went to a sex club years ago and saw something similar. What some guys do is, they cut a tiny nick in their ball sack with the edge of a razor. This is so they can put a straw in it and blow it up. I remember seeing this guy walking up the stairs and carrying his balls like it was a bag of shopping.

RICH: Some blokes fill their scrotums with water as well, so their testicles are essentially floating freely inside their ball sacks.

FRED: People are completely weird, but whatever floats your boat.

RICH: We rarely did the post-gig private party thing, I just thought, 'We're going to get filmed, or beaten up, or something equally unpleasant.'

FRED: If I did anything like that, I'd do it in the safety of my own house, with people I know. There are too many mad people out there.

RICH: There really are – thousands of them. And we seem to have met them all!

Muscles, Drugs and Fucking

Lap Dance Junkie
Fairbrass/Fairbrass/Gray (2001)
Reprinted with permission from FAR Songs

Would you like a little company
Was the first thing she said to me
A baby doll in kitten heels
Gives a look knowing how it feels

So, oh baby, just one more time
This lap dance junkie's spending his last dime
It ain't no joke but I think that I'm broke
Loving you is mentally exhausting

Young assassin dance a while
My cold hard cash for a hot soft smile
I love the tight little dress you wear
I hate you in it when I'm not there
So, oh baby, just one more time…
Never dreamt I was that kind of guy
A hangdog look with those puppy eyes
I guess I'm hooked, can't stay away
A lap dance junkie needs his cabaret
So, oh baby, just one more time…

FRED: I used to go to strip bars a lot, and I'd see the same blokes rocking up the whole time. They would think the girls liked them, and I used to find this fascinating, so I wrote this song. It's written from the perspective of the guys themselves. They get very possessive about these girls.

RICH: As I mentioned earlier, I have a friend who's a hooker, and he confirms this. A lot of the men he meets are married, and they're confused by their situation. They're often in their fifties and sixties: apparently it's not unusual for that age group. Very often, they don't want sex: they just want companionship, and of course they can't tell their wives that they're attracted to men. The lap dance thing is just another way for them to escape.

Chapter 6

Fighting Back

A second bite of the cherry before freedom.

RICH: I presented a documentary called *Naked Eurovision* in Birmingham in 1998, and it was surreal, because in my mind, the experience was largely about failing to get laid. Dana International won Eurovision that year. She was a very cute trans woman, and she made it very clear that I was welcome to spend some time with her in her hotel room, but I was with Stuart and said no. Back in my own room, I was bored, alone and horny, and I thought, 'What the fuck have I done? Saying no was ridiculous.' So I went over to her hotel, but everything was completely dark. The doorman said they'd all gone to bed, so I called a cab and asked the driver to take me to a massage parlour. Off we went to a really shitty part of Birmingham and pulled up outside this place. I got out and the cab drove away – and the next moment, the neon sign outside switched off, because they were closing! I had to walk all the way home to the hotel. It took two hours to get there, and believe me, by the time I got there I wasn't horny any more.

FRED: In 1999, we got a shout from a licensing agent, Bob Cunningham, saying, 'You should come over to the Dance Music Convention in Amsterdam and meet a few labels.'

RICH: Why were we looking to get signed to a label, after the miserable Tug Records experience?

FRED: Well, we weren't completely against the idea of record labels – we just wanted to work with competent people. Anyway, I had a week free, so I went over there and I met with some people from BMG Berlin. They said, 'We think we could work together. Why don't you come over for a meeting at our Berlin office?'

RICH: I remember this. We went over there and met their team and Alex Christensen, who ran a BMG subsidiary label called Kingsize. We played a bunch of new songs for him.

FRED: Kingsize had just released Lou Bega's 'Mambo No. 5', which was a fucking huge record. They had another act called Bell, Book & Candle too, who had had some big records in Germany, so Kingsize was the most successful part of BMG at that time. We signed a production and licensing deal and came in on the back of all that success.

RICH: We had a song called 'You're My Mate' that was just a demo.

FRED: They heard 'You're My Mate' and said, 'That's a hit record.' It's a feel-good song about the importance of friendship when things go tits up.

RICH: It completely reinvented us in Europe. Mind you, they tried to make us change 'You're My Mate' to 'You're My Maid', because they thought nobody knew what 'mate' meant in Germany. We said, 'We're not doing that. The word "mate" is used in Australia and America and all around the fucking world.'

FRED: Alex Christensen took our demo and produced it. The significant benefit we got from him doing that was that he added bagpipes. It turns out that in Hamburg, there are more bagpipe players than in Scotland. It's a weird thing.

RICH: We thought it sounded great, and we liked the dynamics of starting the track with my vocal and your acoustic guitar.

FRED: I remember we were doing a radio show, and on their chart, 'You're My Mate' was number one. After that we went and played a show in this massive sort of Oktoberfest arena. It was huge. So we went on and we started playing the usual songs, and it was going fine – but then we went to 'You're My Mate', and I've never seen a place go so nuts. It was insane.

RICH: It was total mayhem for that three minutes. As I was singing, I thought, 'We've nailed it – this is a real moment.' It was far more rewarding than 'Sexy' from that point of view, because getting successful is hard enough, but bouncing back again is far, far more difficult. The UK music business had already written us off, so this success was particularly sweet.

FRED: Kingsize/BMG understood their market perfectly. They left us alone to write the tracks, and they trusted us to deliver a hit. There was never any: 'Can you send us what you're doing? We need to hear some music.' They just heard 'You're My Mate' once and they knew it would be big.

RICH: Alex Christensen didn't like guitars as much as we did, so there was a bit of an argument over that, but overall, between us, him, Kingsize and BMG Berlin, everything worked really well.

FRED: 'You're My Mate' became a big line-dancing song in Texas, and it was really popular in Colombia and Mexico. It even went Top 20 in the UK, with literally zero airplay. People just liked it. If we'd had radio support, it would have been a big track all day long.

RICH: Kingsize turned out to completely undo all the dislike we'd previously had for record labels – or most of it anyway. What they did, that Tug Records had failed to do, was prepare. They understood what was coming, and they understood how to put everything in place to deal with that.

FRED: So now we were signed to an independent label via BMG, a decade after our first single. In 2001, I was 45 and you were 48 – not the usual career path. Fortunately we looked very pretty.

RICH: We did tons of press for the new album, which we called *Fredhead*. We used to go to Great Ormond Street Hospital, and we'd see kids who had lost their hair to cancer. They referred to each other affectionately as 'Fredheads' because they were bald like us.

FRED: Kingsize set it up brilliantly. The press in Europe were much nicer people than the British lot. Unfortunately, the second single 'Mojive' was rushed, and it's not a track we're proud of.

RICH: We have two or three songs in our career that we refuse to play, and that is one of them.

FRED: It was weird how that song came about. We had a mix of it that we liked, but when we turned up on the day of the video shoot, they were using a mix we'd never heard before.

RICH: We hated it with a passion, to the point where we said, 'Fuck you, and fuck the video too.'

FRED: We should have had some really cool live brass arrangements on there, but they just couldn't be bothered, and we had a bit of a fight about it... business as usual.

RICH: Fortunately, the pre-sales of *Fredhead* were massive, so we didn't give a fuck about 'Mojive'.

FRED: I had no idea that it was going to be as big as it was. I was hopeful, though. I said, 'If the *Fredhead* album goes Top 10, I'll buy myself a Rolex' – and it went straight in at number two. We were in Frankfurt on that day, so I went into a Rolex store and bought myself a watch.

RICH: In the week of release of *Fredhead*, we were headlining at the Schalke stadium in Gelsenkirchen. That felt pretty good for a supposed 'nineties band'.

FRED: That night, we played to 72,000 people in that arena with Lionel Richie. The very next day, we flew to the UK for a radio festival. The presenter said, 'I bet it's a while since you performed to 15,000 people.' I said, 'Yes, it is. Last night was 72,000 people!' Then we did months of shows, Formula 1, award shows and interviews all over Europe. The album went straight to number two in Germany. It was very, very successful and rewarding.

RICH: Germany is the world's fourth biggest record market, and they're also very loyal – so having three Top 10 albums there was a big deal for us.

FRED: If you want to go to a good live event, go to Germany: they're past masters at it. Even their smallest festivals are well organised. I've been backstage at UK festivals and a lot of them need to up their game. In Germany and other countries, they're better at getting the band in and out, and the tech will definitely be better, as will the catering.

RICH: Also, in Germany and other European countries, the promoters will come up and say, 'Thank you for doing my festival.' That's never happened to us in the UK.

FRED: I will say that the *Fredhead* tour was very hard work. Once again, we were shagged out at the end of it.

RICH: Can you see a pattern emerging here?

FRED: We're not lazy, and we're happy to work hard, but fuck me, we got tired.

RICH: In between playing live with the band, we did a few extracurricular projects here and there. I presented a TV show called *The Desert Forges*, which was eminently forgettable. It was shot in Jordan and it was basically a competition in the desert, themed around physical fitness, with different challenges for different people.

FRED: I wasn't invited along, thank God. I do very little TV unless I'm with you. I'm not very good at it, and I'm not the face of the band, fortunately.

RICH: For all the glamour of the shoot in the desert, they could have done it in Kent. I remember we were standing around one day, and the sun was really, really hot, so we were talking about wearing baseball caps. As I walked past the director, I heard him say, 'We can't put Richard in a hat. He'll look like a fucking idiot.'

FRED: Was there anything good about the experience?

RICH: The only good thing about *The Desert Forges* was that I went to that very famous site in Jordan, the Red Fort. We were there on one of the very few days in the last fifty years when it rained, and it was tipping down. Also being driven to the set was cool because the driver played lots of Jordanian songs – stuff I wouldn't normally hear.

FRED: You're good on TV. I always feel like a fish out of water.

RICH: Yes, you have to like all the 'lights, camera, action' stuff to enjoy TV. The reason I love doing live shows is because there's you and the punter, and you can tell straight away if they're into it. You're all there for a good night out. But TV is so controlled. I still get offered a lot of it, but I tend to turn it down, because they're usually cookery things or travel things or stuff that I wouldn't enjoy. I was offered *Celebrity MasterChef* while were doing this book, actually, but I turned it down because it takes up so much time with all the heats you have to do.

FRED: I quite enjoyed some of the TV ads, like the commercial for Meister Proper, which is a German disinfectant.

RICH: Yes, we went to Romania to do Meister Proper. The reason they asked us to do it was because the cartoon character on the label looks a bit like me.

FRED: Wait, it wasn't because of our musical genius?

RICH: Sadly not.

FRED: The early 2000s were a really fun part of our career: 2002 was even busier than 2001. We did lots of TV and we played Popkomm in Cologne, where they closed off the city inside the ring road and put up about thirty stages. It was fucking brilliant.

RICH: We were famous in loads of countries but pretty much forgotten about at home, which didn't bother us.

FRED: In my opinion, that's the perfect situation.

RICH: 'You're My Mate' went straight in at number eighteen in the UK without any airplay. UK radio basically refused to play it, because at the time this country was addicted to monobrow retro-rock care of Britpop. We were just persona non grata.

FRED: Kingsize/BMG Berlin were keeping us so busy outside the UK that it didn't matter.

RICH: We were having far too good a time. We even did what Kingsize asked us to do – well, most of the time.

FRED: We felt that they were on top of it, because they were organising a lot of really good stuff.

RICH: We performed at the 2006 World Cup opening ceremony in front of about 250,000 people at the Brandenburg Gate in Berlin, which was insane. If you want a one-night stand, go to the UK. If you want a long relationship, go to Europe.

FRED: That time was great. It lasted about six or seven years; it was a very good period for us – financially, spiritually and musically. Kingsize/BMG were very supportive and they did a very good job. Fair play to them.

RICH: We recorded another album for them called *Stand Up*, which came out in 2002, with a couple of singles, 'Stand Up (for the Champions)' and 'I Love You (but I Don't Like You)'. 'Stand Up' did really well globally; it's been used in a lot of major sporting events.

FRED: The original idea for 'Stand Up' was inspired by 9/11 and the people who you rely on when things like that happen – first responders, medics, firefighters, police and so on.

RICH: Mind you, I fucking hate 'I Love You (but I Don't Like You)'.

FRED: The production is shit.

RICH: Everything about that song is shit.

FRED: Now I come to think of it, 2002 was a bit of a crazy year. We did a German tour as special guests for Nena. We also went to India as part of a festival sponsored by Pepsi, which was awesome. Larry Carlton was also on the bill.

RICH: I loved India, and I could see why so many British people stayed there. It takes a while to get used to the way they think about life and the afterlife and that kind of stuff. We went to Goa, and we spent a lot of time driving around Mumbai. I've always thought that if you were going to bump into Christ, Mumbai is where you'd bump into him, because it's a very spiritual place.

FRED: The American crew who did all the staging for the Pepsi festival left all their tools and equipment for the local crew, because they didn't have any.

RICH: When we got to the hotel, they'd arranged for an elephant to be there as part of the greeting, and the minute we walked in, the elephant decided to empty its bladder. It went on and on… I thought it was never going to stop – it was a tidal wave of elephant piss. So the magic moment was gone, but we had a good time there.

FRED: We've been back twice, to play at the Bollywood Awards in Mumbai in the early 2000s, which was an amazing experience. The size of the audience was incredible. Over here, you'll go on TV and get three or four million viewers. In India, you ask how many people are watching you and they say, 'Oh, it's probably around 320 million, but it'll be much better tomorrow night because the show is syndicated.'

RICH: We went out to the Caribbean that year too. We were offered a seven-day cruise over there if we played one thirty-minute show on a ship, and we didn't think much about it because we were tired and fancied a jolly. We just thought, 'That sounds cool,' and went over to Barbados, St Vincent, Trinidad and Tobago. It was fun. The only negative thing is when you do a show on a cruise ship, you wake up with the audience. They come up to you at breakfast and critique the show.

FRED: Before we left for the Caribbean, a mate said, 'If you want any coke, I have a good contact in Trinidad.' When we arrived in Trinidad we remembered this, and made a call. To avoid sounding too obvious, I said, 'We'd like three,' assuming we were talking about grammes. He said, 'That'll be 500 Trinidadian dollars.' I thought that was a bit steep, but hey, why not? During our soundcheck we got a frantic call from our PA. She had collected the coke only to find that we'd unwittingly bought three ounces, which is 84 grammes, of very strong cocaine.

RICH: With only three days of the cruise left, we thought, 'What the hell are we going to do with all this gear?'

FRED: We did our best to hand it out, but the cruise clientele weren't very receptive. In an inspirational moment, we decided to decant some of the coke into the salt grinders in the restaurants. Later, we had visions of people saying after lunch or dinner, 'This Caribbean fresh air gives you quite a kick.' The rest of the coke we had to flush away.

RICH: I remember the show quite well, during which there was a storm. We, the audience and the equipment started rolling around a lot. Quite a few people were seasick... we don't generally have that effect.

147

FRED: And 2003 was a busy year. Apart from changing record labels it was Mum's seventieth birthday, so we took her to New York to celebrate at the Waldorf hotel. Early in the flight we noticed the air crew behaving very strangely: one was even crying. Then the first officer announced that the aircraft was under imminent terrorist attack and that we should follow all the crew's instructions. The passengers became very twitchy, and the plane dumped all its fuel and headed back to Shannon in Ireland. When we landed in Shannon, there were police, army and FBI vehicles everywhere. We were told to exit the plane leaving all luggage behind. Our mum, who was partially deaf, was oblivious to the commotion, and peering out of the window, she said, 'I didn't think New York would be so green.' Strangely, this incident was later put down to a customer relations issue, believe it or not.

RICH: Soon after that, you had the serious illness we mentioned earlier.

FRED: Yes – I was so ill that I think of it as a near-death experience. After that I really wasn't up to scratch for a long time, although I thought I was. It took me years to feel better. In terms of feeling healthy, I reckon it was only when we went back on tour around 2016 that I felt fully recovered.

RICH: Do you remember me having to take photos of you in the ICU, as the record label didn't believe me when I told them how ill you were? You've always been a bit peaky, though.

FRED: Well, I was first diagnosed with asthma when I was about seven, and they put me on inhalers, which I still use. Glandular fever in my early teens knocked me for six. Weight training helped when I was older, and I used to inhale steam and frequently used a nebuliser, but I think all the flights and the excessive workload eventually took their toll.

RICH: For some reason, that aircraft experience made me fixated on the idea of buying a Morgan car for about fifty grand. In the end, I bought a Jag.

FRED: The trip to New York and my health problems had quite a profound impact on our thinking. The old adage 'You can't take it with you' came to mind.

RICH: In 2004, we did a song called 'The Wizard' for a film called *Der Wixxer*, which we later found out means 'The Wanker' in German. Why did we do that?

FRED: For the money. It was a cover of a song by Madness, which we liked, and the movie was pretty funny in a slapstick kind of way. It took the piss out of fascism very well. At the eleventh hour one of the stars refused to do any of the agreed promotion for the film. The industry really is populated by a lot of stupid people.

RICH: The downside of Germany is that it's not an influencer by any stretch of the imagination. It influences Austria, because the two countries speak the same language, and to an extent Italy and Switzerland, but certainly not France or England. We had hits in South Africa, because BMG South Africa picked up the licensing. BMG fucked up in other countries because they let their BMG affiliates do soft releases. They should have just said, 'You've got ten days to make your mind up about this release or it's going elsewhere.' So we had Warner Brothers in northern Scandinavia wanting to release the songs, but BMG wouldn't do it because they wanted their local affiliates to do it. We were all very frustrated, because we were getting airplay there.

RICH: We were even approached by LA Reid, the American mogul, who said 'You're My Mate' could be a massive American hit, but he had problems dealing with BMG Berlin. It was an obvious hit: in the American Midwest it was already getting played at line-dancing festivals and country events.

FRED: Anyway, the writing was on the wall in Germany. It was time to move on. We parted ways with Kingsize when they wanted to take over artistic control for the next album. We weren't prepared to do that.

RICH: BMG brought in a new head honcho, who boasted that he couldn't speak any English and had no interest in international artists. As we were their biggest international artist, this didn't feel good. He wasn't even interested in meeting us. We heard he was one of those guys that irons a crease in his jeans.

FRED: Everyone at the label hated him because he was just a numbers man, so they said to us, 'Leave if you can,' so we decided to take their advice.

RICH: Kingsize had an option for the third album, but they had missed the deadline for taking up the option. They phoned Bob Cunningham up and said, 'Let's talk about the album.' Bob said, 'We're out of contract with you: the option has expired and we need to renegotiate. It's not our job to manage your diary.'

FRED: After we left them, Bob started speaking to other people and doing licensing deals. Ministry of Sound were willing to cough up a lot of money just for Germany, so we thought that could be fucking lucrative.

RICH: Our producer Clyde Ward and myself played bass and we all produced the next record, *For Sale*, in 2006. We did most of the recording of the album at our own studio, 2 Blew, in London. The album had a cool version of Peter Sarstedt's 'Where Do You Go to (My Lovely)?'.

FRED: We budgeted the album very poorly; in fact it ended up being our most expensive album since *Sex and Travel*. They wanted a more singer-songwriter type approach, and we didn't know what we wanted. We probably should have pressed pause to think about it. You and I often defer to other people when we're unsure what to do – that's rarely a good idea.

RICH: We were cash rich, because we were doing a lot of shows and bringing back £20,000 to £30,000 every weekend. It was a lot of money, and you think that it's never going to stop. You think there'll be another one next month, and another one and another one. You just get into the habit of this money coming in.

Things eventually went a little bit tits-up with Ministry of Sound. We met the owner once and never spoke to him again. They were a very different animal to Kingsize/BMG.

FRED: We just had a problem with the business. That's all it was. It seemed that wherever we went we were faced with the same problem. We like the music industry, but we're always at odds with the music business.

RICH: So that was it for us when it came to signing to labels. We felt we had exhausted that avenue, so we went back to running our own affairs like we had in the mid-nineties.

FRED: The great thing about being independent and working for yourself is that you don't have a whole bunch of people telling you where to go and what time you need to be there.

RICH: Fortunately, we experienced quite a lot of success, but having run our own labels on and off for many years, we can now see how easy it is for signed artists to get ripped off.

FRED: At many record companies, too much of the money seems to go on interior design, leather chairs, weekend jollies and poor management. That's where a lot of the bands' money is going, because the labels can claim it all as expenses. In our experience, it's reckless to trust the very people we're told to trust: record labels and managers are two good examples.

RICH: That way, at least you know you have a chance of not being ripped off. When it came to relationships with people in the industry, you were always more realistic than me. I was always more about building bridges, at least in the early days.

FRED: I prefer to burn them... There are always downsides, of course. If you run an independent label in the music industry, you will always be marginalised against the major-label cartel. A few years ago, we were shown the voting form for a well-known awards ceremony, and there wasn't an independent label on there. Not one. The awards are owned by the majors, and they're run by the majors, so they control everything.

RICH: We experienced that a little bit with the first Brit awards we were involved in. We were number one in about thirty countries, including the USA and the UK, outselling most of the other nominees by about 10,000 to one, and the only nomination we got was for Best Video. And we didn't even win that!

FRED: The Mercury awards have ignored us too. We had the same problem in Germany, because Kingsize was classed as independent, although it was a part of BMG. They showed me the sales figures: we were outselling Alicia Keys three to one, but she was getting awards coming out of her arse, and we weren't even in the running.

RICH: But we get it – it's like Dustin Hoffman said when he didn't get an Oscar for *Tootsie*. He said, 'You will never get an Oscar for a comedy role.' It's the same for a song like 'I'm Too Sexy'. You might have commercial success with it, which we did, but you won't get any artistic credit for it.

FRED: What we've done since then is sign label service deals, which are like licensing deals. You plug into the mechanism of a label's existing distribution and that can work really well, because these labels have been at it a long time and they've got a fantastic network.

RICH: They work in different ways. Sometimes you'll get a chunk of money, and you spend it how you want and they take a cut;

sometimes the onus is all on you. There are a lot of different deals out there.

FRED: About twelve years ago we went to a lunch event for wealthy City types and corporate people. We chatted with one guy who ran a headhunting company in the City, who was apparently very successful. We mentioned how useless 99 per cent of business professionals are in the music industry, and he said, 'Well, that's because the music industry is not considered to be a serious industry.' I asked him what he meant and he said, 'If we're looking for good people, first we search in the financial sector, and then we go to big tech, big pharma, film and video games – in that order. There's a pecking order, and the professionals that nobody else wants will end up somewhere else – quite often in the music industry. That's why your industry can be a shit show of incompetence.'

RICH: He said, 'There are good people in this country, but not enough. Music is a poorly run industry, because it's generally run by people who couldn't get a gig anywhere else.' In our experience, there's a degree of truth to that. It doesn't seem implausible.

FRED: These people are attracted to the music industry because they perceive it as glamorous. You can be a multimillionaire in some company and there's no glamour attached to that. It's a regular job. You go to the office and you sit at a computer and you make your money and you go home. But there is something very glamorous about standing on the red carpet and waving at people at awards ceremonies. The trappings of it attract them.

RICH: I was stunned at how many A&R guys seem to sign good-looking girls and boys because they want to fuck them. That actually did surprise me. It was the crassness of it. There was no pretence at all. It was just understood.

FRED: We still get labels approaching us. If a label said, 'We want to do an album. You'll have complete creative control, and there's a guaranteed budget for marketing,' we'd certainly be up for that conversation. We're not against it on principle.

RICH: I think the only way to do it would be to meet them at the pub and agree heads of agreement over a cup of tea, and never, ever go to the office. I remember being in the studio and we had an idea for a song. We had a bit of a melody going around, and I said, 'I think this could work in America, with this top line,' and the bloke from Tug Records looked at me and said, 'Fuck America.' I remember thinking that a lot of people on the business side of the industry are seriously fucked up.

FRED: We know a guy at a very successful independent publisher, whose first job was as an intern at a very large independent record label. He told us, no word of a lie, that the label owner called all the staff in on a Monday morning and said, 'This album is our priority. It is going to make or break this label, so everybody's pay will be suspended for the next three months. If you don't believe in this record, and you don't believe in me, please leave the building now.'

RICH: Sadly, we were often seen as a cash cow, and we played that role quite successfully. But we've been over-generous with too many people.

FRED: Lending money to managers, which we've done, is not to be recommended.

Survival Tip No. 12: Watch Your Spending

RICH: When people think you're making money, they hang around you, and at first you think that they're hanging around because they like you – but when the money stops, you never hear from them again. This happens with musicians a lot.

FRED: When you first start off, the music business is such a forest of potential fuck-ups that it's frightening.

RICH: Fortunately, the great thing about getting older is that you can sense people's agenda much more quickly.

FRED: Like alcohol, money and fame can make people behave strangely. Neither my wife Alex nor your partner Stuart were ever seduced by celebrity.

RICH: One of the tricks they pull on you is that when you land in a city to do some gigs and promo, the record company know the route you're going to take from the airport, so they only put your posters up on those roads. So you think, 'Fucking hell, we're everywhere!' But you're actually only on that one road. I swear this is 100 per cent true.

FRED: I guess, like all of us, they've got budgets to watch.

RICH: I think the mistake many people make is that they assume that all artists want the same thing and will do anything to achieve that. Everyone thinks they know who you are. They think they know all about you. As a consequence we're harder than we used to be.

FRED: Much harder. The place that we're in now is much more assertive. We have an attitude now. We really do. That's why I get myself in trouble on Twitter, because there's so much anger on social media. Fortunately, we have a history of having to take care of ourselves in quite hostile places. One guy said online, 'You guys need a slap.' I replied, 'We live in Windsor, come on over. We're not hard to find.'

RICH: Sometimes, if you think you're being kind, people just think you're weak.

FRED: We got ripped off by a promoter in Germany once. The gig was snowed off, so we couldn't play. We met the promoter in the hotel lobby, and he refused to honour the deal, which was that we would be paid 50 per cent of our fee up front, even though we normally ask for 100 per cent. He was really rude to us, and he said, 'Well, you know, it's not a big deal. You weren't our first choice anyway.' So when we got back to London, I made a phone call. A couple of rather unpleasant people visited him, and justice was served. The lesson is that if you fuck us over, you will be held accountable for that.

RICH: It's a cut-throat business, unfortunately.

FRED: I remember Lemmy telling us a similar story once. He told us that a record company were refusing to pay Motörhead what they owed, so he made a phone call, sent some boys round and they got paid.

RICH: We did a TV advert with Lemmy once.

FRED: A bizarre one, on Hampstead Heath, where we were dressed as cowboys. We met him a few times after that and he was always really nice.

RICH: Not at all judgemental, just a nice bloke.

FRED: I dropped off some gear for Motörhead at the Hammersmith Odeon when I was working for Pete Webber Hire. Motörhead were having a quick soundcheck. I've never heard anything as loud in all my life. It was just extraordinary.

RICH: As I've said elsewhere, if you come into the music business from a fairly stable background, with a happy family and good friends, you think the business is like that too. You have to learn that if you're lucky, as we were, family life is a very special place. The wider world is not like that at all.

FRED: We're much more circumspect than we used to be. We don't trust people as readily. You've got to wake up, you really do, which is a shame. At first you think you're more important than the label, but the label's going to be here in a hundred years, and you won't be.

RICH: Whether it's a record deal, or whatever it happens to be, people will tell you exactly what they know you want to hear. Now, I'm aware of that. Back in the day, I used to believe it.

FRED: One thing that surprised us is how compliant other musicians are with their labels and managers.

RICH: They'll do anything, some of them.

FRED: I was stunned at how even well-known artists are so un-questioning and do as they're told. I thought, 'This is bullshit.'

RICH: We did try to do the whole celebrity thing on the red carpet, smiling and waving, but we're just not very good at it. You know, when I see some of the actors and how they use that red-carpet moment, I realise that you have to really want it and you have to be really good at it.

FRED: Do you know the famous line from Rudyard Kipling? 'If you can meet with triumph and disaster and treat those two imposters just the same...' Replace 'triumph and disaster' with 'praise and criticism' and you'll see our point of view. These days I only take notice of my family's opinion.

RICH: I don't think about anyone's opinion apart from ours. If we think something is good, that's important to me. Our studio mate, Jay, has a very good ear for when we get it right. I don't always agree with him musically, but he's got a good ear.

FRED: As brothers in a band, we know that somebody's always got your back. There's a fundamental trust and a shared history, financially and in every other way.

RICH: The only problem with being two brothers in a band became obvious when we went through a period where we needed somebody else in the room to tell us if something was good or not. That's because we tend not to be too critical of each other, so a third brain to view things from the outside would have been useful. That's now changed, as writing as a duo is the norm for us.

FRED: Between *Stand Up* and *For Sale* not much happened because the band was off the road and I was still convalescing. I remember doing some shows around the World Cup in 2006 and I had real health problems. I was wheezing, I had no energy, and my glands kept swelling up every few days, and I'd have to stay in bed. I hadn't realised how much damage the pneumonia and the sepsis had done. After that my consultant suggested I move to Catalonia, Spain, as the air and quality of life is better, which I finally did in 2011.

RICH: We did play the occasional gig, such as one in Russia, which I think was 2007. We decided to do that one because we thought it would be in and out and quite easy.

FRED: Doh! We got that wrong. We were doing this birthday-party gig in Moscow. It was in this ballroom, a massive, beautiful, old-royalty sort of place, but there were only about twenty of them in there, sitting at tables. So we did the show, and got up the next morning, and the tour manager called and said that there was an event happening, a kind of pro-free speech rally.

RICH: We didn't realise that, actually, it was a gay rights event which the mayor of Moscow had not given permission for, so it was illegal. We only found this out too late.

FRED: So we go down there, and we see a whole load of guys dressed in black, wearing facemasks.

RICH: They were some sort of homophobic, anti-gay faction, shouting things like 'If you breathe in poofter air, you will get AIDS,' that sort of thing. They were singing traditional Russian folk songs, and there's loads of cameras and loads of press.

FRED: We jump out of the car, and immediately this does not feel right. This feels very wrong. And the press see us and instantly turn their cameras away from the Russian blokes towards us – so now these guys are really upset because the cameras have stopped filming them.

RICH: We were just standing there while the press were talking to us, and this big guy ran up to me from behind and sucker-punched me in the face. I went down, but only to get my glasses, which had been knocked off, and there was a whole lot of pushing and shoving and jostling.

FRED: I was trying to help you, but I got pinned down. I had bruises on my back and legs afterwards from being kicked.

RICH: I didn't get a chance to swing back at the guy, but I wouldn't have done anyway, because in those situations, if you retaliate, you're fucked, legally speaking.

FRED: We'd been in Russia before, and we knew that the people attacking us were probably off-duty coppers, enjoying their little quasi-Nazi day off.

RICH: The only way we could get out was to scramble out between their legs, which we did. I got free, grabbed my backpack, and said to you, 'Let's get the fuck out.' We called our promoter, and he arranged for us to hide out in a local Italian restaurant that he knew. We hid there for about three hours and then hightailed it to the airport.

FRED: When we got to the airport, we saw the TV and it was all over CNN. I didn't feel safe until the wheels on the plane came up. We had to call Mum before she saw it on TV, as she would have freaked out.

RICH: It was unnerving rather than painful. It just teaches you that some countries are best left alone. Russia is not a place I would ever go back to.

FRED: It's an unhappy place for us, and for a lot of other people. As we write this in the spring of 2022 they've just invaded Ukraine. I remember seeing a TV documentary about racism in Russia, and the interviewer asked some guy about interracial marriages. This guy said, 'It's not natural. When you're washing clothes, you don't put the whites in with the colours.' That's how some people think, and when people are that stupid and narrow-minded, it's best to leave them to it and let them stew in their own juice. You can't talk to them, so it's a complete waste of time.

RICH: When I talked to the press afterwards, I told them that I felt sorry for the loser who had hit me, because of how easily intimidated he so obviously was. In 2012, the *Guardian* sent me on a date with Peter Tatchell, the activist. I liked him. He told me that he got beaten up on the same march in Russia as me, but worse: he got hit on the head so severely that his doctor said, 'Your head may not take another hit like that.'

FRED: What was Peter like?

RICH: Very interesting. I had a long talk with him about what liberation means for gay men. A lot of us feel that we're liberated because we're able to have lots of sex – but that's not what liberation means. True liberation means being able to be honest about the feelings you have for someone and owning those feelings. When Stuart and I were together, we would walk hand in hand in London and I never gave it a second thought, even though marriage was illegal back then. That was liberation, as I see it.

I'm a Celebrity
Fairbrass/Fairbrass/Ward (2009)
Reprinted with permission from FAR Songs

I'm a celebrity
Da de da, da de da

I'm a celebrity,
A five-star fame junkie
I binge then I diet, I vomit on the quiet, I'm a role model, you see
I'm a celebrity
Plucked from obscurity
Now that I'm in it, with my 15 minutes
It's all about me, me, me

It's my life
I dream about it day and night
It's my life
I dream about it day and night
Da de da, da de da da da de da
Da de da, da de da da da de da

I'm a celebrity
You'll find me in the lavatory
I powder my nose, you know how it goes
It's all in my biography

It's my life
I dream about it day and night
It's my life
I dream about it day and night
I'm a celebrity
It doesn't get better, it doesn't get better than this
It doesn't get better, it doesn't get better than this

I'm a celebrity
Unknown sexuality

She shares my limo, but he shares my pillow
Welcome to reality
I'm a celebrity
When it goes tits up you'll see
I'll kiss and tell, they'll all run like hell
Yes, I'm a celebrity

It's my life
I dream about it day and night
It's my life
I dream about it day and night
Da de da, da de da da da de da
Da de da, da de da da da de da
I'm a celebrity

FRED: I wrote these lyrics, as I'm sure is obvious, as a comment about celebrity culture. We're not taking the piss out of the actual people who inhabit that world, although some of them deserve it: it's about the culture itself. The idea that someone can be famous for being famous and the importance that's attached to it. Having been inside that culture, we thought, 'Let's take the piss out of it.'

RICH: 'I vomit on the quiet' is the line that stands out for me.

FRED: Are we celebrities?

RICH: I don't see myself as one, but I think people look at us that way, though.

FRED: We don't play the fame card, though.

RICH: No. We don't demand the best tables at restaurants, saying 'Didn't you watch *Top of the Pops* in 1992?'

Chapter 7

Getting Out

Go indie and save your soul!

FRED: We should probably talk about *I'm a Celebrity... Get Me Out of Here!*

RICH: Oh God, do we have to?

FRED: I think we do.

RICH: 'I'm Too Sexy' gives the impression that we don't take our music seriously. Because of that, we're rarely invited on TV to talk about writing and recording; we're invited onto *Strictly*, or *I'm a Celebrity*, or some travel show. *The Desert Forges* was a good example of that. I was hired as a sort of TV celebrity. Anyway, what the hell – *I'm a Celebrity* asked us to go on the show in 2008, and we were quite into the idea.

FRED: Well, we were tempted by the money.

RICH: And we fancied going back to Oz.

FRED: It was a lot of money, but at the same time, you have to factor in the fact that you might actually win. In that case, you can end up potentially losing work, because whatever you have planned for when you get back – which in our case might be gigs or a tour – has to be cancelled, because you'll be doing promo for the show. You're contracted to do that promo. So all that work gets cancelled before you go on the show, and even if you get voted out and you go home after three days, that work is still cancelled and won't come back.

RICH: The production company's premise was that they wanted to change the format for that year's show. They were going to start the show in the normal way, and then four or five days in, we would just walk up to the camp and join the people in there. Then, and this was the new, clever bit, we'd stay for a few days before vanishing again. The point was to upset the dynamic, psychologically, and make it more interesting for the viewers.

FRED: So we flew over to Australia and they put us up at the Versace hotel, where we had loads of meetings with the health and safety people.

RICH: It's the biggest outside broadcast in the world, and they edit it in real time, with each country taking over from the next. When that happens, the set is made safe for health and safety purposes, so it's swept for insects, all that sort of thing.

FRED: After we arrived, we said, 'So, when are we going into the camp?' and they said, 'Oh, we need about two or three days.'

RICH: We thought okay, and went and lay down by the pool.

FRED: After a day or two, though, we suddenly weren't being spoken to any more. It was very odd. We were just hanging about, with no idea what was going on.

RICH: We knew they definitely intended to bring us onto the programme at first, because we'd had meetings with the health and safety people, and talked with the psychiatrists.

FRED: We were there for a week in that hotel, and then we were taken to Byron Bay.

RICH: We were at this new place for about three or four days, and then we were taken back to the hotel again. By now we'd been there for over a week, and there's only so much lying around you can do before you get bored. We were starting to wonder if they actually wanted us to do the show or not. The whole thing was a shambles.

FRED: I'd smuggled in a phone, and I was in constant contact with my wife, who told me that at first we were being talked about in the press, and that there were rumours that we might go in, and all this sort of stuff. That was all good, but after a couple of days, she told me that they'd stopped mentioning us.

RICH: That's when we started to smell a rat.

FRED: Finally, we tracked down one of the production people, and we said, 'Can someone tell us what the fuck is going here? Are we or are we not doing this?'

RICH: We said, 'Can anyone tell us anything? A phone call? A fucking text?'

FRED: We ended up having a massive row with them.

RICH: I blame the jet lag. Also, we had known before we flew to Australia that we would be expected to take our shirts off in the jungle, so we spent a lot of time training. We'd come off the steroids just before flying in, which didn't help because you get irritable when you withdraw from them.

FRED: We probably had a few glasses of wine too.

RICH: And we hadn't really slept either, because of the jet lag. All of this contributed to us being a little bit touchy, shall we say.

FRED: So we had this giant argument, and they got pissed off at us because we were a bit too vocal, and they flew us home. I admit that we can be a bit of a handful. We get a bit intolerant in some situations.

RICH: The Head of Light Entertainment at ITV at the time called us and said, 'You need to apologise to the production office.' By this time we'd been paid and we'd stopped caring, so we said, 'Whatever. Sorry. We were jet-lagged.'

RICH: At least we got paid.

FRED: It was probably half our fault and half theirs. I think we could have been nicer, and they could have been more professional.

RICH: We found out later the dynamics of the show changed. We were also told that they didn't want 'another' poofter on the show, although we don't know really know what they meant by that. The pursuit of money can take you places you don't want to go. Anyway, we went on to work with a label called Promark in LA, run by a mate of ours, David Levine, where we recorded the album *I'm a Celebrity* to tie in with the show. There was also going to be a new greatest hits album and a remix of 'Sexy'.

FRED: The *I'm a Celebrity* album had quite a good run. It kept us in the limelight as far as 2010 and 2011 due to the successes of the club remixes in the US. We did all the usual TV promo, especially in the USA – VH1, MTV, Good Morning America, Fox TV and TMZ.

RICH: We did all the usual stuff.

FRED: In 2008, we were filming for a TV show in Bulgaria, and we were put in this massive hotel with five hundred rooms, but there was only about fifty people in it, just the film crew and us. When I got back to the UK, I was washing my hands and I could see my skin moving. I thought, 'What the fuck is that?' and went to see my doctor. She said, 'You've got scabies. Have you been sleeping in any nasty hotels lately?'

RICH: My favourite kind of hotel!

FRED: She told me that what they do to save money in these places is wash the bed linen in warm water that isn't hot enough to kill parasites. She gave me this cream, and what's weird is that you can see these things move less and less as the cream gets through and hits them and they die. What often happens is that people often mistake them for heat bumps and they leave them untreated, so they can travel all over your body. For some reason they like to get into your hair. Obviously, for girls that's a nightmare, as sometimes they have to shave their heads.

RICH: We did an album called *Stop the World* in May 2011, accompanied by an acoustic gig at Leicester Square Theatre that we videoed and released on DVD called *Night of the Living Fred*. It's just okay.

FRED: It's a very poorly produced album. There's a complete lack of love in that record, because we bashed it out. Some of the songs we wrote are quite good, but overall, the album doesn't stand up. It's just not good enough. I think we were just a bit out of sorts and our creativity wasn't that high.

RICH: The same year, we released the 'Sexaholic' single. That was licensed worldwide, and it did all right. We shot the video in Amsterdam. I wore a full-body muscle suit that gave the impression that I was naked except for a thong. A little old lady saw me in the street while we were filming – she lost her mind and started berating me.

FRED: We were on Ricky Gervais's TV show too, *Life's Too Short*. At first, we were reluctant to do it, as we always are, and asked who else was on there. They told us that it would be Liam Neeson, Sting and Johnny Depp plus others, so we thought we'd better do it.

RICH: Ricky Gervais and Stephen Merchant are both lovely people too, so we enjoyed it. We asked Ricky why he'd chosen us, and he said, 'I just like working with people that I respect,' which we appreciated.

FRED: From 2010 to 2016 was a difficult period. Your partner Stuart died in 2010, which knocked you for six. Mum's Alzheimer's was progressively getting worse, and we were reluctant to go on the road. We definitely took our feet off the pedal for a while.

RICH: In 2013, I was asked to take part in a gay rights debate at the University of Oxford. I was speaking in favour of gay couples being allowed to raise children. The research I cited indicates that children of gay parents show few differences in achievement, mental function and social function to those of straight couples, and indeed they may also have the benefit of greater open-mindedness and tolerance. I think I did well in the debate, but I have to say, I was nervous.

FRED: You did a good job. This was serious stuff. In fact, there was quite a lot of politics going on in our lives at the time, as there is now.

RICH: Yes, there was. In 2014, we were flown to America to perform on John Oliver's *Last Week Tonight* show, where we did 'I'm Too Sexy for Assad', sending up the Syrian president, Bashar al-Assad, who was apparently a fan of some of our songs. What was interesting was that we got a lot of support from anti-Assad rebels in Syria. We've got a picture of soldiers holding up a big sign saying 'Thank you' and they're literally surrounded by rubble.

FRED: We also attended the anti-Bilderberg demonstrations in Copenhagen in May 2014. For anyone who doesn't know, the Bilderberg Group is made up of elite politicians, royalty, journalists and business leaders who get together behind closed doors and discuss how they think the world should be run. They're not all evil: I think some of them go in with a kind of naivety. These people are now at the centre of the current pandemic, and they have the money and power to try and change the world.

RICH: If you're that powerful, and particularly if you've been elected to power, you have a duty to tell people what you're doing.

FRED: Transparency is essential in that situation.

RICH: We did loads of TV stuff in the early days, but we pretty much say no to everything now. The one thing I did in recent years was just prior to the Brexit vote: it was an arm wrestle with Johnny Vegas. He was a Remainer and I was a Leaver, and we had to arm wrestle on TV to see who would win. It was stupid but it was fun.

FRED: We recorded an album, *Exactly!*, in 2017 and it was issued on an independent label, PMI. We wanted to have someone managing promotion and, stupidly, we paid a manager a retainer. We should have known better.

RICH: We still like this album, but we hit the usual buffers in the UK with TV and radio.

FRED: Taylor Swift's 'Look What You Made Me Do' was released in 2017 and interpolated 'I'm Too Sexy', for which we were well paid: the bump in royalties afterwards was nice too. We never spoke to Her Swiftness directly, but they treated us well.

RICH: That song was huge. I think it still holds a streaming record.

FRED: In 2019 and 2020, we got BMI awards. We had kept touring from 2016 after Mum died right up to February 2020.

RICH: To us, those awards mean validation.

FRED: We've continued to be fairly prolific since then. In 2019, we released two singles, 'Don't Make Me Laugh' and a re-release of 'You're the Best Thing About Christmas'. In 2020, 'Tide' was number one on the Heritage chart which incorporates charts from all over the world. 'We're All Criminals' was written as a response to our lives during 2020. It was also a hit on the Heritage Chart.

RICH: In 2021, we released 'Your Inner Light Is Love'. This track has had great feedback. We haven't been playlisted – except for Radio Jackie – in the UK since the mid-nineties, so we judge a song by audience reaction, not chart positions.

FRED: We think we're in a really good place with our writing and recording.

RICH: Being independent, we don't have to worry about our direction, because we can do whatever we want.

FRED: When you're working with a label, you're expected to have a direction in mind. They expect you to arrive with one ready to go, because they're planning promo and photos and all that stuff. Now, what I like is that we have no direction. If we want to do a reggae track, we can. If we want to do a heavy metal track, we can do that too.

RICH: We perform better these days too. I get nerves about half an hour beforehand, but it's not bad nerves. I know what I am when I'm on stage. I don't become someone else, like David Bowie did, for example. Bowie's thinking with Aladdin Sane and Ziggy Stardust was that he could be more free when he inhabited a character. That's not me. I really like being me the whole time. I've never had any desire to pretend to be somebody else.

FRED: I'm not completely sure about that. For me, there's the onstage Richard and the offstage one.

RICH: Well, maybe to an extent, but they're not two radically different guys. The one on stage is much more fun and much more carefree. And more overtly sexual, I think. I don't mind being sexual when I'm doing stuff like that, but in a jokey kind of way. That's one thing that really pissed me off during the pandemic, because I've really missed that onstage character. He's gone away.

FRED: When we started going back out live a few years ago, we played a tiny little place in Ramsgate where the stage was actually slightly bigger than the audience area. When we walked in, I couldn't believe how small it was, but I remember the gig because I really enjoyed it. It was really sweaty, with people right in your face, and that's how I like it – more like a party than a gig.

RICH: Often the gigs you remember have nothing to do with the size of the venue. For us it's the intimacy we achieve with the audience.

FRED: I wonder what people think of us now, thirty years since we got successful?

RICH: Well, people have got such a bizarre impression of us over the years. Because 'Sexy' was so big, I could invent a cure for cancer and when I die I'd still be the bloke who sang 'I'm Too Sexy'.

FRED: A PR guy that we know was talking to different newspapers about us, and he said, 'Everybody likes you, but you're a bit like the Queen Mother. They like you, provided you don't do anything.' That's why we've had so much flak about the pandemic. People just want us to be there, not to come out and comment.

RICH: You grow up with this idea that if you're an artist, you're kicking against the traces a bit. You're cynical, and you try and see things through your own lens – but the minute you enter into a deal with a major company, you become owned by them one way or another. You have to be independent, if you want to say what you really think. Otherwise, you're just reiterating what someone else wants you to say.

FRED: I quasi-manage the band, I suppose. I handle all the requests, and I tend to come up with ideas – let's try this, let's try that. The success of that setup comes from many, many failures. We haven't had a manager for several years, and we're much happier that way – but if we met somebody that we really liked, and they were committed to us, we'd give them a shot. If they just talked about big deals and big money, that wouldn't be enough – we'd have to like them.

RICH: A lot of artists are incredibly conservative and narrow-minded. They still think that the big deal is the way to go, even though there's ample evidence to suggest otherwise. They'll still hand over their rights in perpetuity, and they'll still hand over a huge percentage for what is basically a bank loan. That's because they feel secure that way. Oddly, we feel insecure that way.

FRED: Well, musicians don't have the dole any more.

RICH: True. The dole was the unofficial arts grant for kids. You have to feed those new musicians, you know – if you want the top of the music industry to be vibrant and interesting, you've got to feed the people who are pushing up from the bottom. You've got to have live gigs, and bands have to be able to cover their costs.

FRED: Drake approached us in 2021 with his song 'Way 2 Sexy', which was like the Taylor Swift song in that it led to a spike in royalties and an awareness that we've been around for a fairly long time now. A lot of the music media reported that Drake had sampled us: there may be a sample in the track, but it isn't us. It occurred to me recently that 'I'm Too Sexy' has been a number one in the US three times now: the original hit in 1991, then with Taylor Swift and now with Drake. You would think one of those hits might merit a Grammy, but there you go.

RICH: We got paid well for usage of that song. I can't remember who said it, but we were told many years ago, to remain solvent in the music business, you have to be making money while you sleep.

FRED: Our writing credits have saved our bacon on more than one occasion.

RICH: In fact, the one piece of advice that I would give to any young musician is to hold on to everything you've got. Nobody's going to do you a favour. What you don't realise when you're a kid and you've got a hit is that other people often just see it as money.

FRED: During the pandemic, our income was hit by over 70 per cent, so when we record music, we have to reduce the number of days we spend in the studio. That means that we have to think carefully about the way we approach the songs: you think harder about what you're doing.

RICH: Fortunately, we're not looking for validation and we've never been particularly motivated by making money. Being independent is the whole point, for us.

FRED: To us, being independent means taking care of business without any help, or without much help anyway. We always had those skills, right from the early days. I think I've always been a bit of a hustler, without even knowing it. It was only when a friend of ours mentioned that to me that I ever thought of myself that way.

RICH: When the band was starting, you were very tenacious, fortunately for us.

FRED: A lot of bands seem to encounter and sometimes create a lot of friction. I think we escape that: people seem to think we're a bit handy because we work out. I also think when we do TV and stuff we come across as pretty affable. We're friendly. We don't bring an attitude to a TV show.

RICH: You've enjoyed having your apartment in Barcelona, as we're relatively unknown in Spain.

FRED: Yes, I like the anonymity – and the weather in the UK does my head in. Our winter effectively goes from the end of October through to April, which is a long time. I like the idea of the South of France, having driven around it a few times. It really is incredibly beautiful. We met lovely people when we used to go to the Cannes Film Festival. Forget the snooty restaurants – if you go back a block or two, it's just regular cafes and the real France.

RICH: In terms of music, I like the idea of writing and recording and releasing songs as often as we like. The trouble is that because shows have stopped, royalties have taken a dip. We aren't super-wealthy, although we are comfortable, so we can't just release songs and lose money for the hell of it. You want your art to be successful too. I feel that most of our songs are good ones. What generally disappoints me with some of our older stuff is the production, especially the Euro-centric production of the Kingsize songs. The recent stuff we've done has a much more international feel to it, and I like the production.

FRED: You and I are huge movie fans, so around 2015 we thought, why not write our own? We presented our idea to a screenwriter and business partner. We've been working on the project ever since. COVID derailed us for a while but we're now back on track.

RICH: In the last seven years, we've learned a lot about the film industry, and have been fortunate enough to be schooled by some very talented and successful people.

FRED: Our acting skills are somewhat limited, but we aren't bad at improv in front of the camera.

RICH: No, although I went to an acting class about five years ago, just to give it a go. I remember we were studying a speech from Shakespeare's *Macbeth*. It's when he's on the heath, and it's all thunder and lightning, and he's going slightly bonkers. I had to learn that speech, and the thing about Shakespeare is that once you get the iambic pentameter rhythm down, it becomes much easier to remember what the words are, so the speech itself wasn't the problem. The problem was that I had to act as the instructor wanted me to act, which was to do this very expressive kind of acting, where you emote to the heavens. But I thought, if it's raining, and it's really stormy, and you're having a mental breakdown, you're much more likely to be huddled up on the ground. At that point I realised that there was no meeting of minds on this, so I gave it up. Anyway, pretending to be somebody else doesn't come naturally to me, which I think is why most pop musicians can't act. They're too busy being themselves and promoting themselves.

FRED: We're used to organising just the two of us most of the time. Trying to co-ordinate all these different factions is like herding cats. Luckily, we know people who are very capable of doing that.

RICH: Talking of the pandemic, I was taken to hospital in 2021. I had fallen over in the bath; I think I like my baths too hot. I remember very little until I managed to let you in.

FRED: I heard a crash, so I went to your bathroom and was banging on the door. I could hear groaning and mumbling inside. Just as I was about to get a hammer, you opened the door – and you were head to toe in blood. A cut in your head was pumping blood everywhere. It took me a moment to understand what had happened, but I sat you down, grabbed a towel and got you to press down hard on the wound. You were in and out of consciousness. On the advice of my daughter, who is a medic, I managed to stop the bleeding and then dressed the wound. You were very disorientated and talking gibberish.

RICH: Not for the first time.

FRED: I became very concerned about the severity of the cut and your mental state, so I called the NHS Helpline on 111. They talked me through it and immediately arranged a doctor to visit. He was great, and having done tests on you, he called an ambulance. During your four-day stay the hospital said you had tested positive for COVID-19 even though you showed no symptoms. I had also tested positive for the virus, but again had few of the expected symptoms. On your return we both took a week out and did a course of Ivermectin, Vitamins D and C, zinc and Quercetin plus lots of rest and water. We were back in the gym within two weeks.

RICH: Predictably, the press and media had a field day – and equally predictably, got all the facts wrong. It was even reported that during my hospital stay I was heard shouting, 'Give me the vaccine, give me the vaccine!' This never happened. In stark contrast, friends and neighbours were very supportive. Any regrets, Fred?

FRED: Do you mean about your bath night?

RICH: No, in general.

FRED: No, not really. The money we're owed annoys me occasionally. We know we won't get it, because one of the companies involved became insolvent and went into administration. Regrets are pointless.

RICH: Like most artists we've been ripped off. We've also made some dreadful decisions, and some really good ones. Focusing on the negative won't create any positives. We tend to be pissed off for a few days, and then we think fuck it and get back to what we believe we're good at.

FRED: So now we do it ourselves. Sometimes we get it right and sometimes we get it wrong. At least we know who to blame.

RICH: What's interesting is that without knowing it, we have become a bit more maverick than we initially were, because in the eyes of the mainstream media we made music for mums and dads. We did what was expected of us: we went on *Comic Relief*, Terry Wogan's show, *The Big Breakfast*, *Noel's House Party* and everything in between. We played the game and then found that we didn't like the game – so we left the pitch and took our ball home.

FRED: Artists often get labelled as 'difficult' or 'divas' – but in reality this often happens because they know what they want.

RICH: That's true. I'm not much of a diva. It's just that if you know what you want, and if you know how you want to work, you're described as difficult. That's all it is, particularly with older artists, who are generally much more experienced than the people around them.

FRED: When we're touring we have one strict criterion: we like to be met by the promoter. This is common practice and a part of the show contract. We also insist on high-quality transport, four- or five-star hotels and business-class flights. If you're going on holiday, you can sit at the back of the plane and get drunk and it doesn't matter – but when you're in and out of different countries, with deadlines to meet, it's a different story.

RICH: I've never said no to an autograph or a photo. The only time I say no is if they ask for one on the way into a show. I say, 'We'll do it after the show,' but we never refuse one point-blank. After the show we always make time to come out and be with the fans. We've always done that from day one. It's important. Unless the autograph is on a penis, which has happened a few times.

FRED: I think we're more complete people now that we're in control of our business. We have a virtual office that filters requests before I see them. We have a PR who handles the requests from the media, we self-release, we self-publish, and we're very hands on. We do run ideas and offers by our PR and our accountant, both of whom we trust. Ideally, I'd rather not manage the band. Tamzin Aronowitz is the only manager we've ever had that added value. If a manager doesn't add value, then what good are they?

RICH: We have to work with the cards we're dealt. Ifs, buts and maybes are no good to anyone.

FRED: We think we're in a really good place with our writing and recording. People often use the word 'heyday' assuming that that is an artist's happiest and most fulfilling time. That certainly isn't the case for us. Our heyday is now. We're independent, self-determining, self-confident and solvent.

Tide
Fairbrass/Fairbrass (2020)
Reprinted with permission from FAR Songs

Tide rolling in

Love, friends and family
Have been so good to me
Wine, food and flattery
Have been so good to me
Little by little 'n' a lot by a lot
Let's be happy with what we've got

Tide rolling in

Life and fantasies
Have been so good to me
Cars, hats and pussy cats
Have been so good to me
Little by little 'n' a lot by a lot
Let's be happy with what we've got

Tide rolling in

Because ya know
You can't take it with you

Tide rolling in

RICH: I love singing the bottom D on this song. The references to 'I'm Too Sexy' are cool.

FRED: We wrote this during Mum's Alzheimer's – it's just about the passing of time.

Chapter 8

Love and Loss

We miss our loved ones – but we're grateful that they lived.

RICH: This chapter is devoted to our parents, to Stuart, who was my partner for twenty-eight years, and to Fred's family.

Peter Fairbrass, 30 March 1921 – 4 December 1988

FRED: We lost Dad at a fairly young age, didn't we?

RICH: We did, sadly. He was overweight, he was a smoker, and his idea of exercise was digging the garden. He was of that generation, you know. I remember him picking me up at the station once and he was tired, looking really red in the face. I remember thinking, 'He doesn't look right,' because he was too florid, and too heavy.

FRED: On the night he died, which was on 4 December 1988, he felt terrible, so Mum called the GP. The doctor went to the house and gave Dad a bit of a check-over and said, 'You're fine,' or words to that effect.

RICH: When Mum woke up in the morning, Dad wasn't there in bed with her. He was dead in the chair downstairs. The cause of death was a heart attack.

FRED: We drove like a couple of maniacs down to the West Country in our old Mini. When we got there Mum was making cups of tea over and over again. She made about eight cups of tea, forgetting the first one.

RICH: It was weird, because we'd thought for some inexplicable reason that it was never going to happen. Dad was still relatively young. I think one of the reasons it didn't knock us absolutely sideways is because we were living in London and we couldn't always afford to visit. If we'd still been living close by, we would have been really shaken. But I think because Mum and Dad were living down in Axminster and we were in London, there was a distance between us.

FRED: I think Dad found our lifestyle concerning. He didn't really connect with us because we had long hair and so on – he was expecting us to grow up suited and booted and in a job. We ended up going to New York, and I think it confused him.

RICH: It would have been good if he'd lived to see the band make it – partly because he felt there's no money in music, but also because we could have discussed the whole gay thing. Presumably, we would have had a conversation about it. I don't know how he would have dealt with that. Maybe he could have dealt with the idea in his head, although seeing Stuart and me together might have been a stretch for him, I think.

FRED: When Mum died, years later, it was a sort of relief because she was so ill, but with Dad, it was just a shock. You can't really process it. It takes you years to get your head around it.

RICH: Dad picked me up at the station once, and as we walked back home, he started quizzing me about Stuart, asking what he did for a living. I think he was putting things together. Deep down, he knew about us, I think. Funnily enough, I think Mum was the other way around. Normally, mothers get it and fathers don't, but when I came out to Mum, she was absolutely crestfallen.

FRED: When was that?

184

RICH: It was a few months after 'I'm Too Sexy' that I came out. I knew that I would have to do it because the band had broken, and I knew it would come out in the press. I'm a hopeless liar with things like that. I just blurted it out, I think. I remember very clearly that we were on the front of *The Sun* that day, and I went into the local newsagents, and I had this vague idea that if I bought all the newspapers in the shop, nobody would know. Of course, then I realised there was more than one shop.

FRED: Mum used to make me laugh: she'd say, 'That Stuart is only after Richard's money.' I had to remind her that you'd been together since 1982, and that up until 1991 Stuart was earning more than you. How did Mum deal with it when you told her?

RICH: She cried for about a year, but I think she wanted to understand what it was about. Dad had gone, and she didn't have a close relationship with the rest of the family, so she felt the need to keep in close contact with us. She was a very loving sort of mother – you know, 'My boys!' To be honest with you, we could have robbed a bank and killed the Queen, and she still would have been proud of us.

FRED: Did you never consider coming out to Dad when he was alive?

RICH: No, for me it was always about whatever made him happy. If he was happier not knowing, then fine. I don't feel the need to be confrontational about things like that.

FRED: Our parents never came to our gigs, partly because it wasn't safe. After the band broke, Mum came a couple of times, but she just started crying because she was so proud.

RICH: Mum enjoyed the fame more than we did.

FRED: I think so. It was a big shift for her, suddenly being the mother of two famous people, particularly where she was living in Axminster, which was a tiny little town. That was a big deal.

RICH: After Dad died, she was single for quite a while, but then she met a guy called Geoff, ex-RAF, quite tall and good-looking. He was a nice guy. They were going to get married, so we went down to Mum's house to discuss the plans. The phone rang, so I picked it up, and it was Geoff, who immediately said, 'Put your mother on.' I handed the phone to Mum, thinking how rude it was that Geoff hadn't said hello, and it turned out that he was in the middle of a heart attack. We all went round to his house, but by the time we got there, the medics were there, paddling him and all that. He died in front of us. That was Mum's last foray into relationships.

FRED: The night before, he had said to Mum, 'When we get married, I'm signing everything over to you.' Sadly, they never reached that point.

Stuart Pantrey, 3 January 1965 – 20 September 2010

RICH: I've had relationships with women over the years, but I tend to connect better with men. In fact, it wasn't until I met Stuart in 1982 that I considered having a relationship with a man. Even then, I was reluctant to admit that was my future, because I'd played around with women.

FRED: Where did you meet?

RICH: When I met Stuart in a bar in Earl's Court in 1982, the band hadn't broken yet, so we fell in love together as ordinary people, without fame getting in the way. He worked at Madame Jojo's, a club in Soho. He was what they call a Barbette, which meant serving drinks, being on the bar and generally entertaining people. I met him in a club, and I'll never forget it. He had just come back from his grandfather's funeral. He had a pair of tight blue jeans on. He had a fantastic pair of legs and was very handsome. Check shirt, hair parted on one side, he looked like a bank clerk, so we got talking. I thought I was dating a pretty straightforward kind of guy, and then I phoned him up the next day and said, 'Do you want to go out?' and he said, 'I'm busy tonight, but you can come and watch me get ready.' I thought, 'Why would I want to watch him put on shirt and trousers?' but I went over anyway. He was going out to see *Cats*, the musical, so he dressed up as a cat with leopard-skin tights, a boob tube, whiskers all over his face and high heels. He told me he was going by bus. I was stunned, but back then he really didn't care about what people thought. That taught me a lot about being true to yourself.

FRED: Brilliant and ballsy.

RICH: Another time, Stuart bought these contact lenses that were completely black, and wore them to a nightclub I was working in. He had bleached blond hair, and he was very pale and skinny, with these black eyes that covered his entire cornea. He came up to me after about an hour wandering around the club on his own and said, 'Everybody's staring at me.' I said, 'No shit, Sherlock – you look like an alien.'

FRED: He often looked fantastic, I remember.

RICH: And he was very honest. You should never, ever apologise for who you are. I used to, and Stuart never did. In fact, on one occasion when he moved to London, he found out that somebody was badmouthing him in his hometown of Basingstoke, so Stuart took the train down there, went to the nightclub where this guy was, bought a pint of beer and tipped it over his head. I thought that was brilliant.

FRED: How did he contract HIV?

RICH: Stuart went out and got drunk and was taken advantage of by some guy: he phoned me up crying the next day. Initially, I wasn't very understanding, because jealousy got the better of me. He went and got a full medical check, and back in those days HIV test results took about six weeks to arrive, so it was then he told me that he was HIV positive. In a bizarre kind of way, him being HIV positive is partly what's responsible for the long relationship. I didn't feel obliged to take care of him, I just felt that that's what partners do. Also, with Stuart's situation, he wouldn't have wanted to go out on the scene again, and have to explain, 'Oh, by the way, are you okay coming back with me, because I'm HIV positive?'

FRED: Do you know who gave him HIV?

RICH: Yes, I think I know who the guy was, and in all fairness this guy may not have known that he was HIV positive. Back then, there were only a handful of people who knew that they were positive. I think he's also passed away now. Stuart was one of the very first people in London to contract it. He must have slept with one of the very few guys in the UK that were positive at the time, back in 1982.

FRED: Fuck – that's incredibly bad luck.

RICH: I sometimes think it's in the stars, that kind of stuff. You can't predict it. There's a great *Blackadder* episode, where the soldiers are in the First World War and they're saying that somewhere out there, there's a bullet with your name on it. Baldrick gets a bullet and writes his name on it and then puts it in his pocket, believing that as it's in his pocket, he won't get shot. It's genius.

FRED: What happened with Stuart after his diagnosis?

RICH: He phoned me up after what appeared to be a nervous breakdown, and I thought he was phoning me to say let's get back together. We met up in Soho, in a pub called the John Snow, and that's where he told me he was HIV positive. At that moment, I absolutely knew that I'd always be there. It was really weird. It never crossed my mind to leave him. I asked him to move into my flat in Putney, and he said, 'I'll move in if you redecorate'! So I redecorated and he moved in, and that was it.

FRED: Did you get on well as flatmates, or did you argue?

RICH: Well, we were patient with each other. I was an arse and so was he, because we were young.

FRED: I do recall a few fireworks now and then.

RICH: Absolutely. As close as Stuart and I were, we drove each other fucking mad. We were very different, and he was very jealous of the band. He couldn't work because he was ill, and I was going all over the world being 'sexy'. It was very difficult for him, and we grew apart, and the sexual part of our relationship went away. He didn't understand the connection between day-to-day affection – normal hand-holding or whatever – and sex. One is an entry to the other. He saw them as two separate things, and I didn't. So without any kind of day-to-day affection, sex didn't follow, for me at least. You need that warmth, and while Stuart was many things, warm wasn't one of them.

FRED: How did he cope with Right Said Fred breaking in 1991?

RICH: I think it must be very difficult when your partner goes from anonymity to being famous. Stuart couldn't work because of his HIV status; he saw himself as being a bit tainted and toxic. I didn't really see it at the time, but when I look back, I think it was a fucking miserable time for him. He didn't make it any easier because his pride got in the way. He struggled with basic please-and-thank-yous. I think he thought it made him seem needy.

FRED: Do you think Stuart would have liked to have been famous?

RICH: I think if Stuart had been a celebrity, he would have loved it. He was in the video for Annie Lennox's song 'Little Bird', because she wanted a double. He wasn't in the business otherwise, although I think he started thinking about it because of what happened with us. I remember him saying to me,

'I think I might want to be a singer.' But he would have been hopeless, because every rejection would have killed him. He was far too obsessed with peer pressure and all that kind of shit.

FRED: Stuart and Mum weren't close for a long time – they were both awkward with each other. Mum was the archetypal jealous mum-in-law.

RICH: I think Mum was jealous of Stuart. She may have thought, 'You made my son gay!', because it had never crossed her mind that I might be gay before I met him. I remember we went to a Chinese restaurant once with Stuart and our mother. Stuart's hair was always absolutely fucking perfect: he had this sort of Elvis quiff at the time. Mum was joking around, and she decided to pull it. You should have seen his face.

FRED: They became closer as time passed, though.

RICH: Mum began to warm to Stuart a little, after a while. We were on holiday, and Stuart used to go scuba diving a very long way out to sea. I remember Mum got very worried about that. But he just wasn't very good at being warm with people. He could be very, very funny, but he wasn't good at being open and emotional. In all the years we went out all over the world, touring and promoting, I never once had a phone call from him. I phoned him, every night.

FRED: Why was he like that, do you think?

RICH: Perhaps because he, his brother and his sister were adopted. When you're very young, you don't remember anything about your natural mother, so you ask yourself why you were rejected or if you did anything to cause it. That's quite a key component of somebody's personality. He didn't want to track down his birth mother: he always said to me, 'She's probably a drunk.' She might well have been, but on the other hand, she might have been a multimillionaire. I think he was afraid to find out, as I think anybody would be.

190

FRED: I remember him having episodes of being extremely ill, and then recovering before getting ill all over again. I don't know how he coped with it.

RICH: When you have HIV, repeated infections are the result of your suppressed immune system. So sometimes he would have a lung infection, or an eye infection. Sometimes he would suffer from some cognitive disability. He was often nauseous. It could be anything, you know.

FRED: I remember once you asked me to pop round as you were particularly concerned about Stuart. He was curled up on the sofa, and I touched him very gently, but he screamed out in pain. I said he needed to go to hospital. I think you'd both got so used to his poor health that you became inured to it. What medication did he take?

RICH: A new treatment, known as triple or combination therapy, came in in about 1996. This was a combination of three or four drugs. With some people, they develop immunity to these drugs over a period of time, and they have to switch it, but that never happened with Stuart. I remember his consultant telling him, 'If you don't take these drugs that I'm recommending, I will never see you again because I will refuse you as a patient. These drugs will save your life.'

FRED: He was very thin at one point, I remember.

RICH: He went down to about fifty kilos or something. In America, when we were out there promoting 'Sexy', he was incredibly thin – really not well at all. He went through a period where he couldn't keep food down, so he had a feeding tube connected directly into his stomach with a pump under the sofa. You filled this thing up with liquid food, and then we'd be sitting on the sofa, watching TV, while this device pumped liquid into his stomach. This was about the time when there was no real empathy to HIV at all. People didn't get it. The mainstream media and the government didn't help.

FRED: There was a break in your relationship at one point.

RICH: There was. I began an affair with Maria, one of our backing singers, around 1999, which continued until 2003. I clicked with her really, really easily. We could go out walking together for an hour or two and not speak, and it was fine. I think she wanted us to grow old together in some kind of summer house in Denmark.

FRED: Then you went back to Stuart.

RICH: We finished it when Stuart had a stroke in early 2003. I was so much in love with him that I couldn't leave him, so Maria and I split up. I told her over the phone, 'Stuart's had a stroke,' and the first thing she said was, 'What does this mean for us?' I remember thinking, 'That's not what I want to hear. What I want to hear is, how can I help? What do you need?' And that's when we split up. Looking back, it was also very tough on her.

FRED: What caused Stuart's stroke?

RICH: He had had two hip replacements, followed by an intense course of steroids. I believe the steroids may have impacted on his bones. The first operation, which I think was his left hip, was fine, but with the second one, I knew something was wrong because his leg swelled up. When you have operations that involve cutting through bone, the idea, I believe, is that your blood should be put through a filter because minuscule bits of bone can get into it. What we think is that with Stuart's second op, they didn't do that, and therefore a tiny bit of bone possibly got into his bloodstream and caused a stroke.

FRED: I remember that – we were in Cologne when you got the call. How bad was it?

RICH: Like most strokes, it was very severe at the beginning. You get a lot of face drop and a lot of paralysis and all that kind of stuff. But if you catch it early enough, which they did, the brain has a really sophisticated way of rewiring itself. When it first happened, his speech was very weird. I remember we were in the hospital, and he said, 'Would you get me some fluffy chocolate?' And I knew he meant ice. I have no idea how I knew that, but I just knew. He couldn't find the right word.

FRED: So you were a couple again after that? I remember you moved to Brighton but Stuart stayed in the London house. You then moved to Chelsea and we bought Stuart his own flat in Fulham.

RICH: Yes, for the last two or three years of his life we were living apart, but I was at his place about twice a week. My feelings about him were the same as they had always been. I knew that I was in love with him, but he had a very low image of himself. I remember saying to him, 'I really enjoy coming to see you,' and he looked at me and said, 'Yeah, right.' He couldn't believe it because he was in a wheelchair and partially paralysed.

FRED: And then, as if HIV and a stroke weren't enough, he got cancer.

RICH: Yes, he was diagnosed with bowel cancer in 2008. We were told it wasn't related to HIV or the stroke. The doctors didn't really know what caused it. It could have been the immune system suppression, it could have been the tablets, or it could have been because people just get cancer.

FRED: That's a horrendous set of health problems to have, especially for a relatively young man.

RICH: He was HIV positive when he was about 19, he suffered a stroke at 35, and then he had bowel cancer when he was 40. So now he was going through radiotherapy and chemotherapy. I think that lasted about a year. You and I went out to Cyprus to record at some point during that period. We were sitting there one evening, and his carer, Doreen, phoned up saying, 'You need to come back to England, because Stuart's really ill.' So we took the first plane out of Cyprus at 5.45 the next morning. I went straight to his flat and stayed with him for most of the weekend. He died at 6.30 a.m. that Monday. Throughout his life, from the age of 19, he'd had regular bouts of ill health. He'd have a good month and then a bad month, often with a variety of opportunistic infections. Stuart had been close to death so many times over the last twenty-seven years that I didn't realise these were our last few days together. We sat in silence for most of that weekend. I was hoping we'd get through it, but I think he was done.

FRED: I remember my wife and I went to see him two days before he died. He started having a conversation with someone who wasn't in the room; he called her Sarah. It was almost as if we had interrupted that conversation – as if our conversation with him was secondary to that conversation. The other odd thing that happened was that one of his eyes started to move independently of the other. It was one of the weirdest things I've ever experienced.

RICH: Some people believe in guardian angels that come to collect you when it's your time. Who knows?

FRED: How did he cope when he learned that the cancer was terminal?

RICH: He was very, very angry about it. He was furious about the way his life had turned out – from his adoption to his illnesses – and he took it out on me and others around him.

FRED: People do that. A friend of mine lost his wife to cancer, and before she died she became incredibly angry about it, and took it out on him.

RICH: It was tough looking after Stuart for that reason. There's a great quote, 'Grief is the price you pay for love', and I think that's absolutely true. He died relatively peacefully, I'm glad to say. I wasn't there, because the carer called the ambulance before he called me, and by the time I got there, around seven in the morning, he had gone. The weird thing was that when he was lying on his bed in his flat, having passed away, he was still present in a funny kind of way. They took about six hours to pick him up, and I spent most of that time in there with him. When they came and collected his body, I refused to watch, because he lived in quite a narrow, small flat, and watching them negotiate him out would have been really, really, horrible, like he was just baggage.

FRED: I remember you calling me and telling me that he had died. I think you were relieved that he was at peace at last.

RICH: That's right. I was pleased for him, in a way, because he was hating his life, and had done for a while, I think. They phoned me up and said, 'Would you like to come and see Stuart laid out in the chapel of rest?' I went, but afterwards I wished I hadn't, because it was a meaningless experience. It's weird: when someone has recently died, their essence is somehow still intact, but this was four or five days later, and it wasn't Stuart lying there. They'd put him in clothes that I knew he hated. Shortly after that, I gave a lot of his clothes away. He had a three-piece suit in a big check, and I gave it to a local charity shop. I was driving past it a few days later, and I got a shock, because standing in the window there was a mannequin, completely dressed up in this suit.

FRED: I remember you had some counselling after Stuart died.

RICH: I did, but it didn't really help. I thought I'd get over Stuart's death in about a year. In the end, it took about ten. In the last year or so, it's finally begun to feel like the Past, with a capital P, because a decade is a milestone of sorts. I think that grief goes much deeper than we think it does. The sense of loss doesn't really go away.

FRED: I hate it when people say, 'Move on.' What does that even mean? You were with him twenty-eight years. Move on from what? It's more to do with acceptance. What do you think you learned from Stuart?

RICH: A lot of things. When we met, I was quite insecure. It was only when I met him and saw how confident he was about being gay, that I began to settle into knowing who I really was. It's weird to look at life in the rear-view mirror, because when you look at life backwards, you can see people for who they really were. I can see Stuart much more clearly for who he actually was now than I did at the time.

FRED: We will never forget him.

RICH: Never. I bought two rings for Stuart and me to wear, and when he died I had them joined together into one, and I wear it all the time. I've reproduced below the eulogy that I read at Stuart's funeral.

Before I start my short story about Stuart, the man whose death we commemorate here today, I would like to relate to you an event which – to me at least – typifies and sums up my wonderful partner, the man I have loved for twenty-eight years, half my life. It was some years ago: we were together. It was a beautiful sunny and warm day in London and, as we had done many times before, we were headed for the Chelsea and Westminster Hospital.

As we slowed towards the lights, Stuart noticed a 'man of the cloth' looking around frantically. He had just parked his car only to realise that he had no money for the meter. Stuart's passenger side window was already down. Leaning out and with a big grin he shouted, 'Where's your God now, then?' We both laughed like drains. I will always remember that moment when I remember Stuart.

Over the years, we loved each other and lost each other in equal measure. The times we had together were wonderful and terrible too. Stuart would not wish me to

196

sentimentalise or romanticise him, his life nor the life we shared. Even now his death is unreal to me, his parting only temporary. I am without an anchor, without a point of reference and without the man I love.

Today, though, I have to put aside my own feelings of loss and tell you about the brave and stoic man whose passing we remember now. The idea of 'love at first sight' was to me little more than a second-rate Tin Pan Alley lyric until, that is, the day I saw Stuart. I can tell you absolutely and without doubt that the very second I saw him, looked him in the eyes and winked – yes, I know winking is a bit naff – I fell completely in love with him.

He was extraordinary in so many ways: beautiful, artistic, loyal and funny. A skilled botanical artist, he was a member of the Royal Society of Botanical Artists and had several exhibitions of his work. *French and Saunders*, the BBC, together with Lily Savage, Jerry Hall and Sting's wife Trudy Styler all benefited from the make-up and hairdressing skills of Stuart. Zandra Rhodes, too, was lucky enough to have Stuart work on hair and make-up for one of her London fashion shows. Possessing the most fabulous pair of legs I've ever seen, he was also a regular performer at Madame Jojo's in the early days when the club was one of the places to visit.

We lived our lives through many enormous challenges. In the early days, Stuart's HIV status provided a gloomy and intimidating backdrop. We did our best. Stuart was brave and consistently resilient. Opportunistic diseases came and went, and we stayed in love, although I do recall a flowerpot hurtling towards me in consequence of something I must have said. Luckily, his aim was not as good as his looks, which explains why and how I can stand here today.

Throughout the eighties, Stuart tried every possible treatment for HIV. Treatments with names and numbers that no one seemed to understand. Mostly experimental, none of them worked. In '91, my own professional life took off. By this time Stuart had lived with the possibility of illness and death for ten years. He was only 28. For him, it must have been both frightening and difficult. I cannot imagine what reserves of strength and determination he must have had to endure as he did. He never complained, whined or pitied himself. He was difficult – yes! He was obstinate – yes! He was argumentative – yes! He was distant, cold sometimes, angry, belligerent, arrogant, bitchy and pedantic. But through it all and despite everything, he was also wonderful, funny, loyal, honest, faithful, clever, witty, talented and sexy. Honestly, what more could a man ask for?

We separated some years ago, about seven or eight, I think. God knows why. For myself, though, deep in my heart I always knew that Stuart was my only love and nothing and no one would or could change that.

We are none of us utterly alone. This is true also of my dear Stuart. He was blessed with friends of great loyalty and love, even if at times he seemed to be the last one to know it. As a friend and carer, Doreen never ceased to surprise Stuart with her love and dedication. Stuart was not an easy person, but Doreen always knew her own heart even if sometimes Stuart did not know his. His life was immeasurably better for having Doreen in it. I must also thank my brother Fred, without whose help Doreen and I would never have been able to care for and support Stuart as we did.

Stuart would be completely knocked out to see you all here today, and I want to thank you from the bottom of my heart for coming here today. I always knew that I would be with him until the end. To see you all here today, too, confirms what I really already knew – that Stuart was irreplaceable, and worth every second of my knowing and loving him.

198

Betty Fairbrass, 15 April 1923 – 4 March 2016

FRED: In the last year or so of Stuart's life, Mum had started to develop dementia, but we had no experience of it, so at first we just thought she was getting old. She started getting really forgetful, so she used to do things like get her front door keys out to remind herself that she was going out to eat. Her apartment was covered in Post-it notes to remind her of phone numbers and pills to take, and so on.

RICH: Eventually, it got to the point where her doctor diagnosed the early signs of dementia. She was about 85 at the time, and she had it for the last seven years of her life, before she died at 92.

FRED: Mum was quite happy most of that time. She did suffer from depression for a while, and we had to step in and get her on some tablets, but that aside, she enjoyed life.

RICH: She stayed in her own home with daily care until it became impossible. We tried to keep it that way for as long as we could, but there came a time when, due to her diverticulitis going undiagnosed, she caught a urinary tract infection and fell and cut herself very badly. A urinary tract infection can cause delirium, which is what happened to Mum. We came to see her in hospital, and we were shocked by the severity of her cuts. Later, we went to her flat and were equally shocked by the amount of blood on her curtains, duvet, the walls and the carpet – it looked like a crime scene from CSI.

FRED: After a few weeks in hospital she moved into a care home. When she left hospital, she thought she was going home, but we knew that was impossible. We took her back to her flat to pick up some things, and she didn't really remember the flat. She remembered certain things in it. We said to her, 'Do you know where you are?', and she did, but only to a limited extent, and then she said, 'I remember being lonely here.'

RICH: I think Mum was quite surprised when we took her to the care home and left her there. I think she was like, what on earth is happening? Initially, she didn't fit in at all, because she was still transitioning into this new place, but within a month or two, she fitted in completely. I find the whole care industry quite interesting. I've often thought I would love to be the CEO of a hospital trust, because I would go to Google and Amazon and Facebook and say, 'If you want, we'll put a huge sign outside our hospital, and we'll say, "This hospital is part-funded by Facebook" or whoever; it'll make you look great. All you have to do is give us a million pounds a year with no strings.' Easy.

FRED: Her fall really accelerated her dementia. When she was up and about again, we used to take her out for lunch, but her tastes and behaviour had changed. She took a sip of red wine, which she'd always loved – and hated it. From that moment onwards we mixed her wine with a little Coca-Cola to sweeten it. And then she stopped recognising food. When there was tomato ketchup and chips at the table, she'd pick up a chip and say, 'Can I put this in that red stuff?' It was very, very odd.

RICH: She also became physically smaller, because she lost weight as her appetite went. People who have dementia badly can't even swallow. It can be terrible.

FRED: We felt bad moving her into the care home, so initially we didn't touch anything in her flat. We just said, 'Let's give her six weeks: maybe it'll be a respite for her and we can take her home afterwards.' That didn't happen, though, because she deteriorated pretty fast.

RICH: She started to look like the other dementia patients very, very quickly. She even found getting into the lift confusing. She started to like having soft toys around, just to cuddle them. The outside world became a complete mystery to her.

One of her favourite sayings was: 'I'm mystified.' She said that a lot, although she also had lucid periods from time to time. There was one occasion when we were sitting in a cafe, and she suddenly passed comment on the newspaper headlines. She was completely lucid for about five minutes. I think of it like an out-of-body experience for her.

FRED: You dealt with it more than I did because I was coming and going from my house in Spain. I felt guilty about that, but I had to do it for my own health, which thankfully did improve a lot.

RICH: The year before Stuart died, her dementia really started to become apparent, which made it a truly miserable time for us. At the same time, we were getting on stage and performing 'I'm Too Sexy'. It wasn't easy, believe me.

FRED: The one good thing about playing those shows is that they gave us, and particularly you, the opportunity to forget what was happening at home for a couple of hours.

RICH: That's true. I also remember some moments that were quite funny. Do you remember when we picked Mum up for your wedding?

FRED: Oh, that was funny. Alex and I met in the King's Road in about 1996. We didn't really date, but we did go out clubbing and to restaurants on and off for about a year. We lost contact in late 1997 when Alex moved to Germany: she'd met a guy and become pregnant. We hadn't spoken for almost five years when we bumped into each other in Terminal 2 at London Heathrow. Her relationship was in trouble, as was mine. We exchanged numbers and she started coming to shows in Germany, as we were on the road a lot at that time.

We maintained a long-distance relationship for about six years, with her in Germany, then Spain, and me in the UK or on the road. We became very close over the next year, so much so that I was introduced to her daughter Marina, who I'm proud to say is now my stepdaughter. The music business being what it is, and me suffering from depression, I have found Alex's support crucial to my mental health and quality of life. That said, the core of our relationship is our sense of humour and our ability to laugh at the world on a daily basis.

As for Marina, I first met her in Stuttgart, in 2003. She was sitting in the back of Alex's BMW X5: she was five years old and looked so tiny – her feet barely reached the end of the seat. Marina and I have forged a very good friendship. We're more like mates than dad and stepdaughter – she has always called me Fred. I am extremely proud of her: she's a lovely human. I'm delighted to say that she seems to have found her soulmate in her fiancé, Scott Palmer.

On 26 July 2010, Alex and I were married in Brighton. She and I have a very tight bond: we see the world very similarly and we have always had each other's backs. I can safely say she is the love of my life.

We got married not long after Mum's Alzheimer's had begun, so when we all turned up to take her to the registry office, Mum was in sweatpants, and said, 'Where are we going? You never told me you were getting married.' I'd told her about it many times, but she'd still forgotten.

RICH: At the care home where she was living, they had a ground floor for assisted living, and the next floor up was for sufferers of what they call 'early to medium' Alzheimer's, and there was a top floor for the more severe cases. We were taken up to see it, because they told us that Mum might end up there. It wasn't a happy place: there were no carpets, because generally the people up there had to wear nappies due to incontinence. I'm very glad she never had to move up there. In the end, she just slipped away in her sleep.

FRED: When you phoned me and told me that she'd gone, although I was really upset, I was also relieved. When we were out with Mum, if she saw a very elderly, frail person she'd always say, 'Promise you'll kill me if I ever get like that.'

RICH: Everyone's been through this. Loved ones die.

FRED: We'll never forget them. Why would we?

We're All Criminals

Fairbrass/Fairbrass/Ward (2011)
Reprinted with permission from Richard and Fred Fairbrass

We're all criminals

There was a time when you could speak your mind down my street
Now that's all gone, cos there's something wrong down my street
It's all signs and parking fines and cameras in your face
I don't recognise this place, oh, it's a bloody disgrace

Can't work, can't play
Can't leave, can't stay
We're all criminals
Can't kiss, can't hug
Can't dance, can't love
We're all criminals, hey

There was a time when there was peace of mind down my street
Now you can break the law before you're out the door down my street
It's all a sham, they don't give a damn, they'll twist the words we talk
Then you'll find yourself in court, if they don't like your sort

Can't work, can't play
Can't leave, can't stay
We're all criminals
Can't kiss, can't hug
Can't dance, can't love
We're all criminals, hey
Hey, we're all criminals
We're all criminals

Can't work, can't play
Can't leave, can't stay
We're all criminals
Can't kiss, can't hug
Can't dance, can't love
We're all criminals, hey

FRED: We initially wrote this about surveillance, and in 2020 we rewrote some of the lyrics to express what we felt about the handling of the pandemic.

RICH: We also love the video that we shot, with Goat Noise Photography.

FRED: These are just cool lyrics with interesting images that I like. The song is about saying that when governments intrude excessively into our daily lives, it can make criminals of everyone. This sounds like a good time to talk about politicians.

RICH: Let's do that...

Chapter 9

Politics and Pandemics

Modern life is rubbish, but it's all we've got.

FRED: Well, where the fuck does all that leave us?

RICH: As we're writing this in early 2022, it leaves us right in the middle of a pandemic. If people are reading this in five or ten years from now, the situation might have improved – let's hope so.

FRED: Let's make our position clear on COVID-19.

RICH: All right then. You and I both tested positive for COVID-19 in the summer of 2021. As I explained earlier in this book, I had been admitted to hospital due to a head injury. During my four-day stay in hospital I tested positive for the virus, although I didn't display any of the symptoms associated with it.

FRED: Same here, although I tested positive at home. As I said above, I rested for a week and was well enough to start training again within two weeks.

RICH: I think that's what people don't understand. Contrary to what has been written and said in the mainstream media, we're not anti-vaccine and we're not COVID deniers – but we are against enforced medical intervention, especially when the vaccine is still in its trial stages.

FRED: The reason this whole thing worries me is that there are some highly qualified people saying, 'This is not right. We're going about this the wrong way.' There's clearly a massive split even within the scientific community, but they're being ignored. The attempted silencing of many scientists and doctors should be of concern to everyone, irrespective of their position. I also think that the pandemic might have reminded a few people about what's important. It's like the old saying, 'The unexamined life is not worth living', which I think is obviously true.

RICH: Absolutely, I think one of our goals as human beings is to bond with one another. Music and sport do that. They join us together on a personal level, which is why the pandemic has been so damaging for many people. It's been all about separation, isolation and fear.

FRED: The absence of shows has been a bit of a headfuck for us. It's a big creative outlet, and I really enjoy that. We didn't do any online shows in the pandemic, because we watched people doing it and we hated it.

RICH: A gig is a tribal experience of one kind or another, and to try and sterilise it in that way is terrible. Also, the audience is a crucial part of the whole thing. Without them, you're taking a really important ingredient out of it.

FRED: So what's the solution?

RICH: In order to get the grassroots live music scene up and running again, you've got to get people happy to stand next to each other, without fear, without masks, shouting and screaming and having a good time, but we've been taught by these governments to be paranoid and fearful of each other. To quote Mark Twain: 'It's easier to fool people than it is to convince them that they have been fooled.' There's a complete absence in government of empathy, love and an understanding of the people they serve.

FRED: That's a bit of an understatement.

RICH: The pandemic has made me realise two things. One is that a lot of artists seem completely owned by the business. The other is that art is one of the few pure things that are left, whether it's writing a book, creating a meal, writing a piece of music or painting a picture. Nobody can fuck with art: there's something really pure about that.

FRED: So let's talk about music and where we're going. Personally, I think some of our best songwriting is in front of us. The pandemic has changed our view of the music industry considerably. We're now more comfortable with ourselves and Right Said Fred, and we're also excited about other projects, particularly our NFT platform.

RICH: We know the 'heritage' music scene is vibrant and that lots of artists are happy working in a retro environment. Although we've dipped our toe into the retro scene, it's not something that drives us. For us, everything is about writing and recording new songs: we don't want to solely perform the back catalogue.

FRED: You play bass and sing regularly, even though we aren't on the road.

RICH: Yes, it's mainly about keeping my voice in shape for the long term. Retaining the tone that you have at the bottom end of your voice, and bringing it into the middle, is tricky – and maintaining that tone in the top end of your voice, for me, is almost impossible. I still take singing lessons from time to time, for simple things like keeping your throat loose and working from the diaphragm. It's a discipline I enjoy. I still love playing bass: all the bass on our new stuff is by me.

FRED: I can tell that some of the musicians we work with and know don't look at us with particularly high regard. They seem to have that music snob thing going on. They were in bands that didn't work out, so they envy our success.

209

RICH: Some of the musicians we know could play our songs backwards. They can tell you what a tritone substitution is – but can't just focus on a simple hook. We know we're not the best musicians, but we can write hit songs and hear a hook, and it seems to drive them fucking potty.

FRED: Just look at the talent shows on TV. Everyone claps when someone hits a high note… what the fuck is that about? The problem with talent shows is that the artist is constantly looking for approval. That's arse about face. The artist should be taking the audience on a journey, not vice versa. The problem with those shows is that they give people the idea that there is such a thing as a good singer. In reality, singing is subjective – it's entirely down to the audience. They either like it or they don't.

RICH: The only thing I would want to do outside entertainment is to own and run a good gym and health club, because that's all about people and healthy relationships, and encouraging people who are nervous about the way they look not to be, so they can get some confidence back. Watching people reinvent themselves through working out is very rewarding. The way we would run it would be to do away with monthly fees: people would buy a certain number of workouts for a certain amount of money and use the gym whenever they felt like it. It would be particularly useful for people who are travelling and can't get to the gym regularly.

FRED: Mind you, we must change old training habits as we get older. I do a lot more stretching and warming up, and I try to keep my reps high and my weights a tad lighter than fifteen years ago.

RICH: True. I have to say, I don't like the lack of energy that comes with getting older. That really bothers me. When I was in my twenties and thirties, I didn't think about getting old at all. It never, ever crossed my mind. Getting old was something

210

that other people did. Now I can see the finish line much more clearly than I could before, because you become much more aware of your mortality as you get older.

FRED: I guess we take fewer risks now, apart from our finances, that is. We do like putting our money where our mouth is.

RICH: Definitely. When I was in college, I had an Austin A35, and so did a friend of mine from college: his was grey; mine was blue. We used to race all the way back from Crawley. The risks we took when we were driving never crossed my mind.

FRED: I don't think about the old days much, but when we're touring, most of the musicians we work with are younger than us, and they're curious – so after a couple of drinks, you end up saying, 'We played with Joy Division, and then I played with Bob Dylan, and Richard played with David Bowie, and then we lived in a crack house,' and they start looking at you in disbelief. Today's music business is far too risk averse.

RICH: Fortunately, we have each other to rely on and we can back up those stories, because we were there at the time. If you don't have the buffer of a family member or a close friend, it's very difficult. I think the mendacity of the people that we worked with really surprised me. If you come from a stable background with loving parents and good friends, you tend to think that the outside world is going to be like that. And it's not: the music business is full of the ghastliest people.

FRED: I wish we'd known that before we got famous.

RICH: I also wish we'd known that there are no rules. When you start off, you think there's a right and wrong way of doing things, and you think you know what you need to learn to fit in. None of that is true. It sounds corny, but you have to stay true to yourself. Write and record what you like, and hope that other people like it too.

211

FRED: What's interesting is that we've had more interest in the UK in the last year than in the previous twenty years. I think it's because we spoke out during the pandemic and stuck to our guns, whereas a lot of other artists didn't.

RICH: I will not say stuff that I don't believe.

FRED: Ah well, that's one of the many perks of being an independent artist. It's been a mad thirty years, but it's been a lot of fun too. I think we've been blessed.

RICH: It's funny how we've changed over the years. I was a recluse when I was a kid, and now I'm more of an extrovert, whereas you've become more reclusive.

FRED: Because of my depression, I have good and bad days. Sometimes I'm just not in the mood for 'Aren't you too sexy for this shop, mate?' Other times I'm fine with it.

RICH: Try singing it every night.

FRED: No thanks, that's your gig. What's left on our to-do list?

RICH: I'd like to record another album. I'd like to keep writing. It's important to me to look for new things. If your mind is closed, that's when you've become truly old. I'd also like to find a house that I would be happy to die in. I've never had that.

FRED: Well, you can't usually choose where you die – although I'd like to die after a really good meal and a good bottle of red.

RICH: That can be arranged.

FRED: Thanks for that. What are we most proud of?

RICH: Putting the plaudits aside, I'm most proud of our longevity. Against all the odds, we're still here.

FRED: God, that must piss off a lot of people.

RICH: Sometimes we're asked to go back and look at our old photos or videos and comment. It can be a tad cringey, but it is what it is. That's what we used to look like – and let's be honest, we were as fit as fuck.

FRED: Yeah, we were – and I'm proud of that. I like a bit of meat on the bone... If I could give some advice to the young Fred and Rich in those videos, I would say, 'Buckle up – it's going to be a bumpy ride.' It's important to learn that the music industry and the music business are two very different animals. The music industry is where the music is written, played, recorded, engineered and produced. The music business is where it can all go horribly wrong.

RICH: Good advice.

FRED: Well, it depends. Before 'Sexy' I might well have said that. By 'Deeply Dippy' we had proved ourselves as musicians, so I probably would have just told myself to get a decent manager and to stay on the road, preferably with the tour sponsored by some major company. That way we could have taken our time over the second album, or just moved on and done a new project.

RICH: I was amazed how fleeting it can feel – that's what really hit me. Once you're in the mainstream, you seem to just go round and around. To me, showbiz is a bit like being on a carousel in the dark. There's a single spotlight, and sometimes you're in that spotlight, and sometimes you're not.

FRED: That makes total sense.

RICH: Thank you...

FRED AND RICH: ... and good night!

Godsend
Fairbrass/Fairbrass (2022)
Reprinted with permission from FAR Songs

Me, I've got a lot to say
What the fuck do I know?
If you wanna walk away
Where the hell would you go?
Going to make today a good, good day
Loving is a godsend

Here we go again, my friend
Never thought it'll come to this, though
If the party ends
Where the hell would we go?
Can we get love to trend?

Loving is a godsend

Me, I've got a lot to learn
What the fuck do I know?
All those bridges I've burned
Where the hell would I go?
When the cold wind blows

Loving is a godsend

I never thought it'd come to this, though
I never thought it'd come to this

Loving is a godsend
Loving is a godsend
Loving is a godsend
Loving is a godsend
Loving is a godsend

FRED: It's a self-effacing lyric, mostly based on my experiences on social media. We've never claimed to be experts so I'm asking, 'What the fuck do I know?' I suppose it's quite a dark lyric, although the music is not.

RICH: It's about love being a gift – and if that's the message you take away from our book, reader, then that's good enough for us.

Acknowledgments

Our family

Betty Fairbrass, Peter Fairbrass, Stuart Pantrey, Alexandra Fairbrass, Marina Schmalzried and Scott Palmer.

Special thanks

Eddie Kidd OBE, Billie Mobayed, Mike Gerrard, Peter Ramsaran at Cousins Brett, Tommy O'Donnell, Peter Gross, Roger Gray, Jason Glover, Rob Manzoli, Steve Tandy, Tamzin Aronowitz, Jenny Roberts at Black Ivies PR, the Champion family at Champion's Farm in Lingfield, Sussex, David Levine at Promark LA and Kay Moreno. Many thanks to Joel McIver, David Barraclough and everyone at Omnibus Press for giving us this opportunity.

Thanks

Barry Gibbons, Mr Prentice (guitar teacher), Mike Day, Peter Webber (Ritz Studios, London), Mrs Sher (our first landlady), Andrew and Dee Dee at the Dance Attic, Clyde Ward, Craig Duffy, Midland Bank (Putney, London), Teresa Pattison, Katie Randall, Andrew Leighton-Pope, Brian Pugsley, Ian Craig Marsh, Andrea von Steht and Heiko Saki Pelka

217

(VSD Hamburg), Bob Cunningham, Jan Dirk Vis and Bas Toemen at Jan Vis Entertainment, Stefan Anowski at Michow Concerts, Stefan Lohmann, Neil Warnock at The Agency, David Gentle, Axel Knigge, Mark Meylan, Penni Harvey-Piper, John Bryan, Graham Bonnet, Annie Fowler, Peter Hawker, Wally Versen, Henry and Fran at Total Records Company, June Honey, Mariya Kaperska and John Carnell at PMI, Mazen Murad at Katara Studios, Dick Beetham at 360 Studios, Kingsize/BMG Berlin, Spirit Music Group, Tug Records, Red Bus Studios, Vinylizor Studios, Abbey Road Studios, Charlie Chandler Guitar Experience, Gibson Guitars UK, Duesenberg Guitars, Faith Guitars, Pigdog Pedals, Analogman, Dave Mason Guitar Repairs, Suzanna Twigg, Goat at Goat Noise Photography, André Selleneit, Carlo Benevento, Ricardo Benevento, Jim, Laia, Jim Jnr and Pablo in Barcelona, Peter 'Little Peter' Barton, Tony Smith at Hit and Run, and Paul Statham.

And an extra thanks to our local community for their continued support and friendship: Richie Micallef, Joanna Levett, Will Mannering, Jean-Baptiste Seguin, Ria Smyth and everyone at Snap Fitness, Tracy and Kate at No. 5, Bente Ottersen, Ellinor Helene Ottersen, Liv Ottersen, Phil Donnelly, Shanel and Jay, Emir Pashaj, Polen Pashaj, Edvin Pashaj, Shaqir Pashaj, Piscopo Giorgia, Salvia Giovanni and everyone at Enzo's Restaurant, Lilly and Adam at Lilly's Cafe, Alper Aslan and Stephane at Monty's Cafe, Abdul Aitbenmoussa at Meimo Restaurant, Katie Young, Ewan King, Grace Rimmer, Karen Page, Earl Newitt, Nick Spooner and South African Matt.

Musicians and crew

George Brinkhurst, Paul Pearson, Pete Hopkins, Phil Spalding, Jocelyn Brown, Sally-Ann Marsh, Dawn Knight, Dean Howard,

Acknowledgments

Denise Modjallal, Nadine Rönnebeck, Trevor Barry, Raphael Ravenscroft, Chuck Sabo, Kat Deal, Phil Taylor, Mark Price, Gordon Davies, Ray Weston, Dzal Martin, Gerald Elms, Jon Howells, Dominic Glover, Jonny Brister, Maria Kofoed, Ulrich Rhode, Henning Brandt, Matthias Meusel, Marcus Gnadt, Emre Acka, Ivo Vossen, Steve Hughes, Stuart Calder, Clare Partington, Stefan Basford, Joy Rose, Louise Clare Marshall, Carsten Gräser, Mike Rose, Gary Jones, Sam Hickling, Ryan Burnett, Jodie Scantlebury, Simon Taylor, Darrin Mooney, Rich Milner, Terl Bryant, Emily Dolan-Davies and Tommy D.

Charities we have worked with

Homeless Worldwide, Stroke Association, St Mungo's, Crisis, Hunger First, Alzheimer's Society and HIV research.

Rest in Peace

Craig Duffy, Brian Howe, Fred Kobler, Little Peter, Michael Eckstein, Mike Day, Molly Duncan, Chris Ridge and Chrissy in NYC.

Joel McIver thanks

David Barraclough and the team at Omnibus Press, Tommy O'Donnell, Steve Tandy, Andy Knight for photography, Simon and Fenella at Stable Cottage in Otterton, and Kirstie at the Kings Arms for the loan of her umbrella.

No thanks to

A small number of individuals who seriously ripped us off, and we do mean seriously – to the tune of millions of pounds. Jazz Summers was one of them, but he's dead. The others are still around. You know who you are.

Final Statement

Doing what we want, in the way we want to do it, is more important to us than money or fame.

Survival: A Poem

From time to time it's good to stop, count your blessings
Underline the good things. It's too easy to focus on the negative
Contrary to popular belief we consider ourselves blessed
Killjoys are ten a penny
You have to surround yourselves with positive thinkers
Only then can you reach your potential
Ultimately it is of course down to the individual
Grab it like a rabbit, don't be deterred
Uncertainty, fear and doubt are the foundation of failure
Yammers are a distraction, keep them at bay.

About the authors

Richard Fairbrass and Fred Fairbrass are multi-platinum and award-winning songwriters who have scored number one hits in many countries, including three US number ones, three UK number ones, and a number one in Japan. They were the first band since The Beatles to reach the number one slot in the US with their debut single and have won two Ivor Novello Awards for songwriting and three BMI Awards. They have performed for the Queen, at the Bollywood Awards and at the 2006 World Cup in Germany, their global sales total 30 million, and their songs have been streamed over 100 million times on Spotify. Elements of 'I'm Too Sexy' have influenced songs by Taylor Swift and Drake in recent years, leading to a new generation of Right Said Fred listeners.

Joel McIver is the author of 35 books on popular music. He often appears on TV, radio and podcasts.

Index

All songs and albums are by Right Said Fred, except as stated.